THE BRIDGE OF PROGRESS

Lancaster Bridges Book Two

Sylvia Price

Penn and Ink Writing, LLC

Copyright © 2023 Sylvia Price

All rights reserved

This is a work of fiction. Names, characters, places, and incidents are either products of the author's imagination or are used fictitiously. Any similarity to actual events or locales or persons, living or dead, is entirely coincidental.

No part of this publication may be reproduced, stored in or introduced into a retrieval system, or transmitted, in any form, or by any means (electronic, mechanical, photocopying, recording, or otherwise) without the prior written permission of the copyright owner. The author acknowledges the trademarked status and trademark owners of various products referenced status and trademark owners of various products referenced in this work of fiction, which have been used without permission. The publication/use of the trademarks is not authorized, associated with or sponsored by the trademark owners.

CONTENTS

Title Page
Copyright
Stay Up to Date with Sylvia Price
Praise for Sylvia Price's Books
Other Books by Sylvia Price
Unofficial Glossary of Pennsylvania Dutch Words

Chapter One	1
Chapter Two	17
Chapter Three	28
Chapter Four	43
Chapter Five	52
Chapter Six	64
Chapter Seven	77
Chapter Eight	88
Chapter Nine	100
Chapter Ten	113
Chapter Eleven	126

Chapter Twelve	138
Chapter Thirteen	146
Chapter Fourteen	161
Books By This Author	171
About the Author	183

STAY UP TO DATE WITH SYLVIA PRICE

Subscribe to Sylvia's newsletter at newsletter.sylviaprice.com to get to know Sylvia and her family. It's also a great way to stay in the loop about new releases, freebies, promos, and more.

As a thank-you, you will receive several FREE exclusive short stories that aren't available for purchase.

Porsche's
INTUITION
A Jonah's Redemption Story
SYLVIA PRICE

HOPE
for Hannah's
LOVE
Amish Love Through the Seasons
SYLVIA PRICE

SYLVIA PRICE
EVE
AN ELIJAH COMPANION STORY

PRAISE FOR SYLVIA PRICE'S BOOKS

"Author Sylvia Price wrote a storyline that enthralled me. The characters are unique in their own way, which made it more interesting. I highly recommend reading this book. I'll be reading more of Author Sylvia Price's books."

"You can see the love of the main characters and the love that the author has for the main characters and her writing. This book is so wonderful. I cannot wait to read more from this beautiful writer."

"The storyline caught my attention from the very beginning and kept me interested throughout the entire book. I loved the chemistry between the characters."

"A wonderful, sweet and clean story with strong characters. Now I just need to know what happens next!"

"First time reading this author, and I'm very impressed! I love feeling the godliness of this story."

"This was a wonderful story that reminded me of a glorious God we have."

"I encourage all to read this uplifting story of faith and friendship."

"I love Sylvia's books because they are filled with love and faith."

OTHER BOOKS BY SYLVIA PRICE

Sarah (The Amish of Morrissey County Prequel) – FREE
Sadie (The Amish of Morrissey County Book 1) – http://getbook.at/sadie
Bridget (The Amish of Morrissey County Book 2) – http://getbook.at/bridget
Abigail (The Amish of Morrissey County Book 3) – http://getbook.at/morrisseyabigail
Eliza (The Amish of Morrissey County Book 4) – http://getbook.at/eliza
Dorothy (An Amish of Morrissey County Christmas Romance) – http://getbook.at/dorothy
The Amish of Morrissey County Boxed Set – http://mybook.to/morrisseybox

✸ ✸ ✸

The Origins of Cardinal Hill (The Amish of Cardinal Hill Prequel) – FREE
The Beekeeper's Calendar (The Amish of Cardinal Hill Book 1) – http://

getbook.at/beekeeperscalendar
The Soapmaker's Recipe (The Amish of Cardinal Hill Book 2) – http://getbook.at/soapmakersrecipe
The Herbalist's Remedy (The Amish of Cardinal Hill Book 3) – http://getbook.at/herbalistsremedy
The Amish of Cardinal Hill Complete Series – http://mybook.at/cardinalbox

❊ ❊ ❊

A Promised Tomorrow (The Yoder Family Saga Prequel) – FREE
Peace for Yesterday (The Yoder Family Saga Book 1) – http://getbook.at/peaceforyesterday
A Path for Tomorrow (The Yoder Family Saga Book 2) – http://getbook.at/pathfortomorrow
Faith for the Future (The Yoder Family Saga Book 3) – http://getbook.at/faithforthefuture
Patience for the Present (The Yoder Family Saga Book 4) – http://getbook.at/patienceforthepresent
Return to Yesterday (The Yoder Family Saga Book 5) – http://getbook.at/returntoyesterday
The Yoder Family Saga Boxed – http://getbook.at/yoderbox

❊ ❊ ❊

The Christmas Cards: An Amish Holiday Romance – http://getbook.at/christmascards

✻ ✻ ✻

The Christmas Arrival: An Amish Holiday Romance – http://getbook.at/christmasarrival

✻ ✻ ✻

Seeds of Spring Love (Amish Love Through the Seasons Book 1) – http://getbook.at/seedsofspring
Sprouts of Summer Love (Amish Love Through the Seasons Book 2) – http://getbook.at/sproutsofsummer
Fruits of Fall Love (Amish Love Through the Seasons Book 3) – http://getbook.at/fruitsoffall
Waiting for Winter Love (Amish Love Through the Seasons Book 4) – http://getbook.at/waitingforwinter
Amish Love Through the Seasons Boxed Set – http://getbook.at/amishseasons

✻ ✻ ✻

Jonah's Redemption: Book 1 – FREE
Jonah's Redemption: Book 2 – http://getbook.at/jonah2
Jonah's Redemption: Book 3 – http://getbook.at/jonah3
Jonah's Redemption: Book 4 – http://getbook.at/jonah4

Jonah's Redemption: Book 5 – http://getbook.at/jonah5
Jonah's Redemption Boxed Set – http://getbook.at/jonahset

❊ ❊ ❊

Elijah: An Amish Story of Crime and Romance – http://getbook.at/elijah

❊ ❊ ❊

Finding Healing (Rainbow Haven Beach Prequel) – FREE
Finding Hope (Rainbow Haven Beach Book 1) – http://mybook.to/rhfindinghope
Finding Peace (Rainbow Haven Beach Book 2) – http://mybook.to/rhfindingpeace
Finding Love (Rainbow Haven Beach Book 3) – http://mybook.to/rhfindinglove
Finding Home (Rainbow Haven Beach Book 4) – http://mybook.to/rhfindinghome
Finding Joy (Rainbow Haven Beach Book 5) – http://mybook.to/rhfindingjoy
Finding Faith (Rainbow Haven Beach Book 6) – http://mybook.to/rhfindingfaith
Christmas at Rainbow Haven (Rainbow Haven Beach Book 7) – http://mybook.to/rhchristmas

❊ ❊ ❊

Songbird Cottage Beginnings (Pleasant Bay Prequel) – FREE

The Songbird Cottage (Pleasant Bay Book 1) – http://getbook.at/songbirdcottage

Return to Songbird Cottage (Pleasant Bay Book 2) – http://getbook.at/returntosongbird

Escape to Songbird Cottage (Pleasant Bay Book 3) – http://getbook.at/escapetosongbird

Secrets of Songbird Cottage (Pleasant Bay Book 4) – http://getbook.at/secretsofsongbird

Seasons at Songbird Cottage (Pleasant Bay Book 5) – http://getbook.at/seasonsatsongbird

The Songbird Cottage Boxed Set – http://getbook.at/songbirdbox

* * *

The Crystal Crescent Inn (Sambro Lighthouse Book 1) – http://getbook.at/cci1

The Crystal Crescent Inn (Sambro Lighthouse Book 2) – http://getbook.at/cci2

The Crystal Crescent Inn (Sambro Lighthouse Book 3) – http://getbook.at/cci3

The Crystal Crescent Inn (Sambro Lighthouse Book 4) – http://getbook.at/cci4

The Crystal Crescent Inn (Sambro Lighthouse Book 5) – http://getbook.at/cci5

The Crystal Crescent Inn Boxed Set – http://getbook.at/ccibox

UNOFFICIAL GLOSSARY OF PENNSYLVANIA DUTCH WORDS

Ach – Oh
Aenti – aunt
Amisch – Amish
Appeditlich – delicious
Bruder – brother
Daed – dad
Danki – thanks
Eldre – parents
Englisch/Englischer – non-Amish person
Familye – family
Gaern gschehne – You're welcome
Gmay – local Amish community
Gott – God
Gude daag – Hello (literally Good day)

Gude mariye – Good morning
Gude nacht – Good night
Gut – good
Kapp – Amish head covering
Kinner - children
Kumm – come
Mach's gut – Make it good (a parting phrase)
Maem – mom
Nee – no
Nochber – neighbor
Onkel – uncle
Schweschder – sister
Willkumm – welcome
Wunderbaar – wonderful
Ya – yes

CHAPTER ONE

"I'm glad she's gone."

Samuel Stoltzfus grunted in response. He didn't need to ask to whom his younger brother, Levi, was referring; it was obvious.

His appetite expunged, Samuel placed his fork down on his plate, leaving his breakfast largely untouched.

Levi continued eating, oblivious to anything being amiss.

Samuel knew that Levi had not intended to be deliberately cruel, but his words stung like a sack of salt poured over a gaping wound.

He didn't agree with his brother's sentiment but also didn't want to argue. It was pointless because *she* had chosen to go. Despite Samuel's wishes otherwise.

She was Hannah Fisher—the woman Samuel

had hoped to marry. But she decided to leave their Amish community to continue attending college instead.

While he supported her right to choose her own path, it was not one they could walk together, which forced him to finally acknowledge that they had set their sights on very different things in life.

Samuel desired a traditional life with a wife and children. And as difficult and heart-wrenching as it was, he'd had to face that Hannah wanted something else. Something more than him and what he could provide for her.

When she left at summer's end, he vowed to find a way to let go of the future that he'd envisioned for them—a dream of a future that he witnessed shrinking more and more as its probability of coming to pass decreased—until it became but a pinprick on the horizon.

It had taken Samuel a long time to acknowledge the truth and to accept it; his heart was a number of paces behind his brain and initially refused to believe what was inevitable.

Believing and accepting the hard truth was one thing, but moving past his feelings for Hannah was proving to be arduously difficult and painful. Not because she had an unbreakable hold on his heart.

True, Hannah's leaving had hurt immensely, but his heart was not irreparably broken in the process.

The real reason he was finding it so difficult to move forward was that he feared opening his heart once more to the possibility of making a life with someone else, only to be crushed yet again. He didn't think he had it in him to endure it all over again and come out on the other end with his heart intact.

A sharp screech pealed through the silence as Samuel pushed his chair back from the table and its wooden legs protested against the plank floor. He carried his plate and deposited his plate in the sink, the clatter of the sturdy china dish against the porcelain basin echoing loudly in the hushed kitchen.

"I'm going into town to pick up a few things." Samuel moved toward the back door and grabbed his hat and coat from their usual hook on the wall.

Levi nodded in acknowledgment but didn't speak.

Donning his hat, Samuel swung open the farmhouse door and walked out, pulling it to swing shut behind him.

As he descended the back stairs, the bottom one dipped beneath his weight, reminding him that he needed to stop in at the hardware store while he was in town to buy some boards to replace the rotted step.

Samuel had meant to take care of it for a while, but other chores took precedence—first, the harvesting of the crops, and then the repair of the barn roof before Lancaster County received its first snowfall of the season.

The morning air was crisp with a nip still lingering from the previous night, and he paused to slip on his coat. A slight breeze rustled the tall winter-brown grasses and the few leaves still clinging stalwartly to the trees.

Breathing in the scents of the land that had been in the Stoltzfus family for several generations, he took a moment to savor and appreciate the beauty that surrounded him, giving silent thanks for all the blessings in his life.

The late autumn sun cast its bright rays over the rolling hills that formed a patchwork of pastures and fallow fields, their boundaries marked by wooden fences.

Samuel and Levi had been fortunate to have a good harvest that would see them well provided for through the coming winter.

It's so easy to allow disappointment to overshadow all the good in my life. Gott, *please help me to focus on the many things I have to be thankful for rather than the one thing that didn't turn out as I'd hoped.*

Samuel resumed his trek to the barn, homing in on the chirping of birds filling the air and allowing their symphony to lift his spirits.

The livestock had already been tended to before breakfast, so he led the horse from the stall and hitched it to the buggy before climbing into the driver's seat and taking hold of the reins.

The horse obeyed his click-of-the-tongue command, and the buggy lurched slightly as it was set in motion. The crunch of the wheels on the hard-packed dirt and the clippity-clop of the horse's hooves thudding along the rutted path that led to the road into town created a rhythmic tempo.

The countryside on both sides of the dual-lane highway was scattered with farmhouses and barns. Here and there, clusters of pine trees provided some protection from the wind for cows that had been turned out to graze on the last bits of browning grass before winter blanketed the landscape with snow.

The peacefulness of the journey allowed Samuel's mind to wander. He cherished the simplicity of their traditional way of life, tending the land with his brother. But that did not stop him from yearning to find a woman who could be a partner for him—someone with whom he could hopefully have a family of his own one day.

As Samuel neared the outskirts of town, the farms were replaced with houses situated closer together on smaller plots of land. Landscaped yards took the place of open fields and pastures, and he caught glimpses of clothing hanging on lines to dry. Children played in the yards, their melodiously joyful laughter ringing out and bringing a smile to Samuel's face.

As he steered the horse down the town's main street, he recognized the familiar faces of friends and neighbors going about their daily business and exchanged nods of greeting with them.

The mouthwatering scent of freshly baked bread wafted from the local bakery, which he intended to make his second stop. But first, he needed to see to his errand at the hardware store.

Pulling up in front of the hardware store, which was located a few blocks past the bakery,

Samuel drew back gently on the reins to bring the horse to a stop. He disembarked from the buggy, his sturdy shoes landing on the cracked pavement.

When he entered the store, the owner called out a cheerful greeting, which Samuel returned before making his way to the lumberyard out back where he could find the wooden boards he needed to repair the damaged back step at the farmhouse.

Once he had gathered the necessary supplies, he returned to the front of the store to make his payment. He exchanged a few pleasantries with the owner as the older man rang up the items and completed the transaction.

With his errand at the hardware store finished, Samuel returned to his buggy outside and loaded the wooden boards inside. He then settled into the driver's seat once more to make the short trip to the bakery.

The warmth of the Lapps' bakery interior was a sharp contrast to the cold temperature outside as Samuel stepped in a few minutes later. He doffed his hat and breathed in deeply, inhaling the delectable aromas. The scent of freshly baked bread and sweet pastries hovered thickly in the air.

Scanning the familiar surroundings, his eyes fell on someone he had not expected to see.

Lydia.

Lydia Lapp had been Samuel's childhood friend when they attended the local Amish school together. But then her father passed away, and her mother moved Lydia and her two younger brothers to another community to be closer to the children's maternal family.

It had been years since Samuel last saw Lydia. He didn't know that she was back in town. He wondered when she'd returned—and how long she would be staying.

Was it just for a short visit? Or longer?

Lydia was standing behind the counter where a variety of baked goods were displayed on shelves in the glass case, talking with her aunt, but the sound of the door closing behind Samuel drew her attention. It took only a moment for recognition to light up her gaze, and her lips curved up in welcome as she called out a greeting to him.

Lydia had a natural radiance about her that hadn't been there when they were children.

Or maybe I just didn't take the time to notice it since I was always so enamored with Hannah Fisher.

Lydia's golden-brown hair was pulled into a bun anchored at the nape of her neck and covered by a traditional *kapp*. Delicately arched eyebrows framed blue eyes that reminded Samuel of a cloudless summer sky. Her slim figure was clothed in a dark gray dress with a white apron overlaying it.

Fond memories of their childhood friendship came to mind, and he realized that he had never truly forgotten her despite the passage of time.

Warmth spread through his chest as he approached the counter. "*Gude mariye*, Lydia." He took a moment to politely greet her aunt as well before directing his focus back to Lydia.

He beheld her, his open gaze taking in the sight of her. A soft blush suffused her cheeks at his unspoken admiration. A dozen questions filled his mind, but he couldn't seem to voice any of them.

"How can we help you, Samuel?" Mrs. Lapp asked, breaking the silence. "Your usual order of freshly baked bread?"

"*Ya*," he replied. "And can I also get a cinnamon roll? I'm afraid I didn't take the time to eat much at breakfast this morning."

Lydia reached for a box to begin packaging his order, but her aunt nudged her aside to take over the task. "I'll see to that. Lydia, why don't you take a break and catch up with Samuel," the older woman suggested with a wink.

Lydia's pink-tinged cheeks flushed red with slight embarrassment at her aunt's not-so-subtle matchmaking attempt. But she was curious about what had happened in Samuel's life during the time she was away, so she didn't protest.

There was an air of quiet confidence about him, an assurance that came from a life rooted in faith and tradition.

His eyes, a rich brown hue the color of melted chocolate, seemed to pull her in. His warm gaze revealed genuine pleasure at seeing her again, and she felt her cheeks heating for an entirely different reason.

When he entered the bakery, he had removed his hat to reveal dark brown hair with just a slight wave. It framed his face, adding a touch of softness to his rugged features. His skin was tanned from his work outside, and despite only being in his early twenties, the beginning of fine lines radiated from the corners of his eyes when he smiled.

He wore dark trousers and a solid-colored button-down shirt beneath a sturdy coat that emphasized his broad shoulders.

Lydia was a year Samuel's junior. Although they were friends as children, she hadn't seen as much of him after he left school at fourteen to help on his family's farm. Then, a few years later, her family moved away from the area after her father's passing. Before his death, he and his elder brother, Henry, had co-owned the bakery.

Plating a cinnamon roll for Samuel and another for herself, Lydia rounded the counter and carried the plates to a nearby table, then settled into the chair across from Samuel.

He removed his coat, draped it over the back of his chair, and sat down, taking a bite of his cinnamon roll.

Aunt Martha appeared at Lydia's side with two glasses of milk. She set them on the table and then rushed off to see to another customer.

"It's *gut* to see you again, Samuel," Lydia said once the older woman was out of earshot. "How have you been?"

"*Gut*," he replied. "Levi and I keep busy on the farm."

"How are your *maem* and *daed*?" she asked.

"They were killed in a buggy accident several years ago. It's just me and Levi now."

"*Ach*, I'm sorry to hear of your loss. I—"

He quickly changed the subject as though not wanting to dwell on the tragedy. "What about you, Lydia? What brings you back to town?"

"I've moved back here to help my *aenti* and *onkel* with the bakery."

After several years of living in a more progressive Amish community, Lydia returned to Lancaster County to help Henry and Martha Lapp. The older couple was getting on in age, both approaching sixty, and had no children of their own to take over running the bakery. Neither of Lydia's teenage brothers had been interested in moving back to take on the responsibility.

Even Lydia hesitated to make the move at first. The decision to leave her mother and brothers and return to her childhood community had been difficult, but she knew it was the right one.

As she sat there with Samuel, laughing and reminiscing about their past adventures, Lydia found herself feeling a spark of hope that her return to the community was not only a chance to help her aunt and uncle but also an opportunity to renew the bond she'd once shared with Samuel.

The bakery bustled with activity as customers came and went, but Lydia barely noticed. She had been picking at her cinnamon roll as she talked to Samuel, much more interested in their conversation than the delicious treat.

After they had caught up on what happened

in each other's lives over the last few years, the topic shifted from their personal experiences to the changes that took place in town while she was gone.

Many people welcomed Lydia back, just as Samuel did. But she noticed a reserved attitude toward her among some. When she questioned her aunt about it, the older woman told her not to worry about it. But it continued to percolate in the back of her mind, and she decided to raise it with Samuel.

"There has been growing tension between the traditional and more progressive factions in our *gmay*, with *nochber* taking sides against each other," he explained. "An *Englisch* company has been buying land just outside of town for the past year, and now there's talk that they are planning to build a factory on the site. It's a controversial issue since many *Amisch* are opposed to any sort of change and view the increased encroachment of the outside world on our daily lives as a threat, while proponents argue that it will bring economic opportunities to our town."

Lydia couldn't help but notice the concerned tinge in Samuel's voice as he spoke of the challenges they faced, and she felt compelled to try to reassure him. "Change is inevitable, but perhaps there is a way for us to find common ground to preserve our traditions while still being open to allowing progress which could benefit our *gmay*."

"If there is, we certainly haven't found it yet. And I worry that this latest issue will cause our *gmay* to become irreparably divided," Samuel admitted.

Given how long-lasting the conflict had already been, could Lydia possibly be able to help bridge the two sides? Or would her opinion just be one more voice added to the cacophony of unresolved disagreements?

She determined she would learn more about the plans for the factory in hopes of finding an answer. Although she was suddenly encountering problems in the Lancaster County community that she hadn't expected, seeing Samuel again cast a whole new positive light on returning to her former hometown.

Lydia looked forward to renewing their friendship.

And it perhaps becoming something more.

❊ ❊ ❊

Samuel, reluctant to say goodbye to Lydia, reminded himself of chores he still needed to see to at his farm, meaning he couldn't linger any longer at the bakery.

But he was already anticipating their next meeting!

"I'm sure I'll see you again soon," he said in parting.

A smile curved up the corners of Lydia's lips as she nodded. "I would enjoy that, Samuel."

After leaving the bakery, he climbed into the buggy, his gaze pulled inexorably back toward the glass storefront window for one last glimpse of Lydia. He met her gaze as she looked back at him.

Samuel tipped his hat to her, then urged his horse forward, setting the buggy in motion.

Samuel felt drawn to Lydia in a way he had not been when they were friends in school. But this magnetism he felt towards her was tempered by wariness of putting his heart on the line once again at the risk of being hurt again.

The yearning of Samuel's heart for a partner with whom he could build a future, someone with whom he could find a connection and who would complement his simple Amish life, with strong roots anchored in faith and tradition, was intense, but he also couldn't deny the presence of the vultures of fear that preyed upon his fledgling hope.

Is this Gott *guiding me and directing my steps toward Lydia?*

The conversation had flowed easily between them as if the years apart were mere weeks. There was an effortlessness in being with her, a familiarity due to shared memories and unspoken understanding.

Samuel's thoughts drifted back to Hannah, the woman he once hoped to marry. Though he had struggled with her departure when she decided to leave to continue her education, after spending time with Lydia, he realized he'd found solace in their rekindled friendship.

Is it possible for me to forge a new path? One that could lead to a future I've never considered before?

CHAPTER TWO

Lydia attended the church service that Sunday morning with her aunt and uncle. It had been a couple of days since her unexpected reacquaintance with Samuel, and her heart fluttered like a butterfly on a sunny day at the thought of seeing him again.

Her eyes scanned the room, assessing the familiar faces and the subtle changes that were visible in the friends and neighbors she remembered from her childhood. She spotted Samuel sitting on the far side of the room with his younger brother, Levi.

When Samuel noticed her looking in his direction, a warm smile spread across his face, brightening his brown eyes. She reciprocated his smile.

Levi ignored her, looking past her, but perhaps he just hadn't seen her. Or didn't recognize her now that she was no longer a child.

Lydia had always known Levi to be solemn, somber, and quick-tempered, but there was an additional air of austerity etched into his expression that piqued her curiosity.

Was it the pain of losing both of his parents that led to this harshness I can read in his demeanor and body language? Or is it something more?

She couldn't shake the feeling that there was an underlying tension between the two brothers for some reason.

Forcing her gaze away from the Stoltzfus brothers, Lydia caught sight of David Lantz. Over the course of the last week, she had learned he was a regular customer at her aunt and uncle's bakery. Lydia felt a sort of kinship with David, who also spent several years living away from the Lancaster County Amish community. Unlike Lydia, however, he had spent his time in the *Englisch* world before returning to the area the previous spring and recommitting himself to the Amish faith and way of life.

Throughout the worship service, Lydia struggled to keep her thoughts on the sermons as her gaze seemed to shift toward Samuel again and again without her conscious volition. Several times, he caught her stare and her cheeks would heat with a slight blush.

She found comfort in the familiar hymns and the sense of unity that filled the home of the family that was playing host to that week's gathering. At the end of the service, as her aunt and uncle visited with some friends, Lydia felt an invisible pull toward Samuel that she couldn't explain or disregard. But she didn't try to fight against it and excused herself to approach him.

After exchanging greetings, they lapsed into momentary silence before both started to speak at the same time. Lydia stopped speaking just as Samuel did likewise, and another few seconds of silence followed until they broke into simultaneous laughter.

After their chuckles subsided, Samuel waved for her to go ahead. "You first," he insisted.

They stood together by the edge of the gathering, where they could speak freely without concern of their words being overheard by others. Not that Lydia was worried about eavesdroppers. But she liked the idea that she and Samuel shared something that was theirs alone—even if it was nothing more than a simple conversation.

"What did you start to say a minute ago?"

Samuel prompted.

"I just wondered when I might see you at the bakery again."

"I usually go into town every Friday morning to run errands, which always includes a trip to the bakery."

Lydia worked in the mornings, so there was no chance that she might miss him. She wouldn't have hesitated, though, to ask her aunt for a different shift had that been the case.

Samuel's expression turned serious. "There's a community meeting planned for next week to discuss the proposed construction of the factory in our town. I fear it's going to exacerbate the discord between the two sides."

She could sense Samuel's genuine concern for his community's well-being. Yet, at the same time, a part of her couldn't deny the potential benefits that the factory might bring. "I understand your reservations and respect your viewpoint, Samuel. But we must also consider the changing needs of our *gmay*. The factory could provide opportunities for greater prosperity for many. I'd like to come to the meeting and hear what others have to say. Perhaps we can find common ground and work toward a solution that will ensure our values and traditions are respected while embracing the changing world."

Lydia considered the responsibility she felt toward the local Amish community. She prayed for wisdom and guidance, knowing that the path ahead would be rocky, uphill, and convoluted. But as long as people were open-minded, she was confident that they could find a way to navigate the challenges ahead.

Levi approached them at that point and pulled his brother away on the pretext that they had chores waiting for them back home.

It was likely true, but Levi's reserved attitude toward Lydia gave her the impression that it had also been an excuse to separate Samuel from her.

Or perhaps I'm letting my imagination run away with me and I'm seeing things that aren't really there.

After the two men were gone, Lydia continued to dwell on her conversation with Samuel.

Even though she knew that difficult decisions would have to be made, she was ready to face them alongside Samuel and the others in the community. She was grateful for the connection she shared with him in their rekindled friendship —and hoped to explore the possibility of turning it into something more.

* * *

Samuel sat on the buggy seat, the leather reins gripped tightly in his hands as the horse trotted along the familiar country road toward their farm. The autumn sun, though it provided scant warmth, shone brightly overhead.

Samuel's encounter with Lydia after the church service stirred up unexpected feelings. Uncertainty settled heavily upon him, his mind preoccupied with thoughts of her.

Samuel had avowed to move past his improbable wish of marrying Hannah Fisher after she left their community to continue pursuing a college education. Since he was an adolescent, he yearned for a wife who would be content living a traditional Amish life and raising a family with him. When Hannah's departure turned those dreams to dust, it left him guarded and wary.

The rekindled comradery and strong pull he felt toward Lydia, although stirring a semblance of excitement in him, made him more cautious than thrilled, especially because her progressive views could clearly prove to be a hindrance to anything more than friendship between them. The thought of enduring another agonizing heartache similar to the one he'd experienced when Hannah left had Samuel questioning whether he could risk opening himself up again when it might only lead to further disappointment.

Levi shifted on the buggy seat beside him, and Samuel tried to push away such grim thoughts. "I don't think you should be acting so friendly with Lydia Lapp."

Samuel, surprised that Levi's thoughts seemed to be traveling a path similar to his own, turned to look at his brother with a raised brow. "Why not?" he asked even though he could easily guess the answer.

Levi's expression hardened. "After living in a more progressive New Order *gmay* for so many years, there is no doubt that Lydia will have changed, becoming overly influenced by modern ideas and turning away from old traditions. I predict she'll try to bring about change here, but I aim to ensure that she doesn't succeed."

Samuel's grip on the reins tightened, his knuckles paling. "You don't know that for sure."

"And you don't know that it's not so," Levi countered.

Will Lydia try to make changes? Just as Hannah

attempted to do before deciding on leaving our gmay *to continue her education instead?*

Levi turned his head, his distrustful expression meeting Samuel's contemplative gaze. "I know Lydia used to be your friend when you were *kinner*, but she's been gone for several years, and you don't know her anymore. I wouldn't be so quick to grow close to her again if I were you." He reached out, placing a hand on Samuel's shoulder. "I don't want to see you hurt again, *bruder*. Don't let your heart be swayed again by someone who may not hold the same beliefs and values as us."

His younger brother's words echoed his own reservations, and Samuel felt suddenly breathless —as though his chest were being constricted by unseen coils of fear. The pain of his failed courtship with Hannah gripped his heart, squeezing it and serving as a stark reminder of the potential hazard of pursuing a woman who did not hold the same traditional views as him.

I can't bear even the thought of going through such heartache again. But is Levi's warning solely borne out of concern and protectiveness for me? Or is it instead prompted by his opposition to any sort of changes away from our traditional ways?

Samuel hated doubting his brother's motives,

but Levi's past actions made Samuel question just what the younger man was capable of—and how far he was willing to go to ensure that things stayed the same in their community.

The rhythmic clip-clopping of the horse's hooves accentuated the silence between the brothers. Samuel stared ahead of him but didn't take in the sights and sounds of the countryside as his thoughts remained introspective.

His heart, still bruised from Hannah's desertion of sorts, was a tangled mass of contradictory emotions. He yearned for a wife and children, to settle down and live out the rest of his days as a husband and father, but his fears of being forsaken again held him back.

Should I guard my heart against developing any deeper feelings for Lydia? Or am I just borrowing trouble and in danger of passing up the opportunity for the kind of loving partnership I've always dreamed of? Am I judging Lydia unfairly because of the hurt I suffered in what happened with Hannah?

Samuel was in a conundrum: he didn't want to take a step in the wrong direction, but he needed to start moving in some direction in order to figure out his next step. Otherwise, he would continue to remain stuck, going nowhere.

He considered that after feeling the sting of disappointment with Hannah with respect to romance, it might be prudent not to rush things with Lydia without first taking the time to determine whether their hopes, plans, and dreams for the future were aligned.

Will Lydia soon begin to feel stifled here after living in a more progressive New Order gmay? And more specifically, with the kind of traditional life I seek?

He prayed for a sign from God to guide him in the right direction.

The bitingly cold wind sliced through him, and Samuel shivered. He huddled forward as he pulled on the reins to steer the horse onto the rutted dirt track that led to their farm. His turbulent thoughts came to a stop at the same time that the buggy came to a halt near the large barn behind the house, and he hopped down from the seat.

Samuel had reached a decision. He would take time to discover who Lydia truly was. That was the only way to know for sure whether there might be hope for them being anything more than just friends. Until he figured that out, it would be sensible not to pursue anything more than friendship or to cultivate his seedling affection for her. Lydia deserved the opportunity to be assessed by her own actions rather than Samuel making assumptions about her based on Levi's or anyone else's observations.

There was no denying that he felt drawn to Lydia, like a bee to honey, and wanted to spend more time with her. But it would be with purpose: to get to know more about the person she had become as an adult—and whether she was still the same kind, caring, and loyal girl he used to know.

Perhaps it's worth the risk of hoping if the reward is that I'll finally find true happiness.

Samuel had much to think about. Still, he could not ignore the way his heart beat a bit faster in anticipation at the thought of seeing Lydia again soon.

CHAPTER THREE

Lydia had arrived just as the community meeting was starting, so there wasn't time for her to speak with Samuel beforehand. However, she had spotted him the instant she walked through the door. She might have gone to sit beside him except for the fact that Levi occupied one of the chairs next to him and she wasn't sure that Samuel's brother would welcome her company.

Instead, she took a seat in an empty chair near the back of the room and listened as the first person began to speak about the purpose of the gathering.

"We've come here to discuss the factory that an *Englisch* company plans to build on land outside of town," an older man said.

Lydia recognized him as the owner of the buggy shop in town and a member of the Amish school board. Abe Troyer was known to hold more progressive views—unlike many of his generation.

"We must consider the impact the proposed factory will have on our way of life, our families, and the environment," Mr. Troyer continued. "I expect there to be much debate, but I hope we can avoid any hostility or raised voices during this meeting. Although we don't expect to decide on anything tonight, I'd like everyone who wishes to speak to have a chance to voice their opinions."

Lydia was eager to hear the discussions surrounding the *Englisch* factory, a topic that was rumored to have sparked considerable dispute among the community members already. She'd overheard much talk from the bakery's patrons over the past few days.

The meeting had drawn a considerable crowd, and it was clear from their expressions—furrowed brows and fierce frowns—that many were concerned about the effects of the outside world further encroaching on their town.

Given that the more traditional members held a strong conviction for preserving their way of life and were resolute in their determination to maintain the simplicity of Amish traditions, it was not surprising that change, especially of that magnitude, was met with skepticism and fear from many.

Voices rose in dissent, expressing concern about the potential pollution, the disruption of their agricultural practices, and a host of other possible negative consequences. The contentious topic revealed the deep rift that had emerged within the once close-knit community that Lydia remembered from her childhood.

"The factory will bring unwanted changes," Levi Stoltzfus proclaimed, indicating that members of the older generation were not the only ones determined to cling to strict tradition in their daily lives.

"It's already causing further division within our *gmay*," someone else added.

"I've seen the detrimental effects factories have had on other towns," a gray-haired man spoke up. "We risk losing our connection to the land and our self-sufficiency."

One by one, other members rose to share their opinions about the factory's potential impact on their Amish traditions and concerns about the environment.

Lydia listened intently, her gaze shifting between the speakers. She understood their desire to protect their way of life. But she couldn't help considering the potential benefits the factory could bring.

When Samuel stood up to speak, her focus sharpened on him. As a boy, he displayed a steadfast commitment to tradition and unwavering devotion to their community. She didn't expect that had changed.

Samuel's words confirmed as much when he expressed his opposition to the *Englisch* factory. "We must consider the adverse effects this factory will likely bring. Our simple way of life, rooted in faith and tradition, may be irreparably altered."

His words resonated with many in the room, eliciting nods of agreement and murmurs of support.

Lydia felt pulled from two sides, like a medieval victim having their limbs wrenched from either side to the point of dislocation by The Rack. Although she understood their doubts and trepidation, they were only considering the possible downside of the proposed factory with no thought for the potential benefits.

After living in a New Order community for several years, Lydia had a different perspective. But she absolutely agreed that all sides should be heard and considered, and she prayed that common ground would be found.

As the discussion continued, Lydia, from her advantageous standpoint, weighed the arguments from both sides. She acknowledged the importance of preserving their Amish values and safeguarding the environment. Yet, she also recognized the possible positive effects the factory could offer—a chance for economic growth, job opportunities, and a way to secure their community's future.

She rose from her seat to voice her own views. All eyes turned to her, people twisting around in their seats to see her at the back of the room, and she felt somewhat daunted to be the focus of attention in such a large group. She felt Samuel's gaze on her but forced herself not to look at him for fear that she wouldn't be able to follow through on speaking words that were in direct opposition to the opinions he'd expressed but a few minutes before.

Lydia took a deep breath to steady herself before starting. "I understand the concerns and reservations many of you have expressed about the factory and the changes it may bring. Our *gmay* is deeply rooted in simplicity and harmony with nature. But we must also acknowledge the changing world around us."

Whispers of dissent spread through the room.

But Lydia pressed on, her determination unwavering. "I believe that we can remain true to our values even as we adapt to the changing times. The factory presents the possibility of numerous new opportunities for our *gmay*, not just for ourselves but for future generations. It can provide economic support for our families through additional jobs. It could bring new resources and advancements that may benefit our farming practices and enhance our quality of life."

Some nodded in agreement as Lydia spoke, while others frowned, clearly unconvinced.

David Lantz stood to add his voice in support of hers. "I believe that we can find a way to embrace progress while still honoring our heritage. We can ensure that any changes are in line with our beliefs and do not compromise our way of life."

Murmurs of dissent continued to ripple through the crowd, and Lydia noticed that a number of expressions remained troubled or uncertain. Her heart felt conflicted, knowing that her vocal stance challenged the deeply ingrained views of the more conservative members of the community. She understood the opposition, the fear that allowing any sort of change could threaten their traditions. But she also saw the potential for prosperity that lay before them if they embraced new ideas.

"We can work together to set guidelines to ensure the factory aligns with our values," David continued. "Progress doesn't have to come at the expense of our faith or traditions."

As the meeting continued, the opposing opinions didn't decrease. Rather, an equal number argued just as strongly for compromise as against it. Lydia's words, along with David's and others, had offered an alternative perspective to the issue at hand.

She respected those who were outspoken in their opinions opposing the factory, knowing that their motivation was to protect their community and preserve their traditions. Yet, she remained resolute in her own belief about the potential benefits and opportunities that could be provided by the proposed development in the area.

Lydia considered the potential consequences of her supporting the factory and their implications.

It has set some of my nochber *against me and might even cause Samuel to distance himself from me,* she thought sadly.

But she held steadfastly to her conviction that their community could adapt without losing the most fundamental aspects of Amish life.

One thing she knew for certain as the meeting drew to a close was that change would not come easily. The council meeting was adjourned without any consensus having been reached, and the community members began to disperse, still talking and arguing among themselves.

Since Lydia had been seated near the back of the room, she exited before Samuel, and he wondered if she would still be lingering outside by the time he made his way through the clusters of people to reach the door.

As he stepped out into the chilly evening air, close behind Levi, Samuel paused to look around. He was relieved to find that Lydia had not yet left despite the unwelcome discovery that the two of them were on opposite sides of the fence.

Without a word to his brother, Samuel moved toward her. She greeted him with a warm smile, obviously undeterred by their differing views.

Samuel was firmly opposed to a factory being

built in their community. Yet, Lydia's wise words lingered in his mind, challenging his staunch resistance. He admired her ability to consider the potential benefits, but that didn't change his own beliefs—nor his reluctance to embrace ideas that deviated from the familiar.

The memory of the pain of Hannah's choice to leave the community rose within his chest, leaving him cautious about investing his heart in another woman who held progressive views.

Lydia's open-mindedness and willingness to consider the benefits of the proposed factory sparked more than a little apprehension within him. He had witnessed firsthand the strained relationship with his brother that the tension between tradition and progress caused over the past year, and he feared a recurrence if he allowed his heart to be swayed by Lydia's perspective.

Samuel glanced around at the others who had not yet departed. None seemed happy with the outcome—or lack thereof—of the meeting. He noticed Levi staring in his direction with a grim frown but ignored his brother's dark look.

He turned his gaze back to Lydia. "I'm worried about how divided our *gmay* is," he confessed.

Her eyebrows knit together, indicating she

shared his concern. But her words bore more optimism than her expression. "It will take time to change people's minds."

Whose minds is she referring to? The traditionalists? Or the people like her who are in favor of progress?

Samuel knew that Lydia's opinion on the matter and his own were at direct odds. He did not want to argue with her, however, so his reply was noncommittally vague.

Lydia didn't seem deterred by his lack of obvious agreement. She added, "I understand others' hesitation. Change is a difficult thing to accept, especially when it challenges personal viewpoints. But sometimes it's necessary. I'm not suggesting we abandon our traditions. I believe there's a middle ground—a way to preserve our values while also embracing progress. We can work together to prevent any negative impact on our way of life while also benefiting from the opportunities that new businesses can bring to our town by establishing agreements with the *Englisch* that respect our traditions and values. Finding a middle ground or compromise isn't that new a concept, actually. I mean, our *gmay* allows us to use a phone in times of emergency even though we don't believe in owning one. That's an example of holding to tradition but taking the good from an outside influence."

Her ideas held merit, and he couldn't deny the truth in her words. Perhaps there was a middle ground that could form a bridge between their Amish community and the outside world.

Samuel and Lydia disagreed because their individual perspectives were shaped by their own experiences and convictions. But her explanation opened his eyes to new possibilities, challenging his preconceived notions. He had always been taught to resist the influences of the outside world and hold tight to Amish traditions. But Lydia's words forced him to confront the rigidity of his own thinking.

He had much food for thought. Part of him wanted to cling to his reservations, to guard his heart against truly considering her progressive ideas and risking floundering in the quagmire of confusion, indecision, and possibly heartbreak. But another part of him longed to find a way to bridge the gap separating their differing beliefs.

Can Lydia and I ever see eye to eye on this issue? Can we navigate the challenges that lie before us and find a way to preserve the essence of our

Amish community while embracing opportunities of the outside world?

Samuel's uncertainties and questions still plagued him, but he knew that he couldn't let fear dictate his actions. He parted ways with Lydia when she indicated that it was time for her to return to her aunt and uncle's home.

After she had left, Samuel was left standing alone with his thoughts. He couldn't deny the impact Lydia had had on him, the way her words chipped away at his skepticism. He questioned his own stubbornness, realizing that being open to new ideas didn't mean abandoning his values but rather finding a *balance* between tradition and progress.

Samuel resolved to attend the next community meeting with an open mind, ready to listen to different perspectives and seek common ground. He knew that change would bring its own set of challenges, but he felt a glimmer of hope within himself—a hope that they could bridge the divide not just between Amish and *Englisch* but between him and Lydia as well.

His optimism quickly dimmed when Levi appeared beside him, his expression even grimmer than it had been a few minutes before.

However, his younger brother didn't voice what was on his mind until they were seated in their buggy and headed back home to their farm.

He knows I'm rendered helpless to listen to him, unable to avoid his words while we're confined in the buggy, Samuel thought to himself.

"I think you should stay away from Lydia," Levi declared, folding his arms across his chest. "She'll fill your head with her modern ideas and cause you to rethink your own beliefs."

Samuel didn't think he could stay away from Lydia even if he wanted to—which he didn't. But he didn't admit as much to his brother.

And how does Levi know that I felt swayed by Lydia's words? Are my feelings written across my face?

Samuel kept his gaze fixed on the dark road ahead rather than looking at his brother and risking his expression revealing anything more to Levi.

Still, he couldn't stop himself from defending Lydia. "She values our way of life and only seeks to find a balance between tradition and progress."

Levi scoffed and retorted in a voice tinged with bitterness, "We've already seen what happens when you become entangled with a woman who questions our traditions. It leads to division and heartache."

As hurtful as Levi's malicious gibe felt, there was no denying the truth of his remark, so Samuel remained silent.

"I think we should actively block the construction of the factory," Levi opined after the silence in the buggy had stretched on for several long uncomfortable moments.

"The building plans haven't even been approved by the town council yet," Samuel replied, welcoming the subject change, however slight.

"I have no doubt it will happen soon," Levi commented. "But that doesn't mean I intend to allow *Englischers* to further encroach on our *gmay* without a fight. Standing idly by while an *Englisch* company starts building a factory in our town will lead down a dangerous path, blurring the lines between our Amish way of life and the outside world, pulling more and more of us away from our traditions."

"Perhaps at the next meeting—"

Levi slashed a hand through the air, cutting off Samuel's words. "Talking does nothing but widen the rift in our *gmay*. We talk and talk, but nothing is ever resolved. There comes a time when action must take the place of endless discussion. Actions, not words, have more impact in making people see the error in their way of thinking."

A sudden jab of fear at what Levi might decide to do pierced Samuel, but he tried to push such worry to the recesses of his mind and turn his thoughts back to Lydia instead—which was a much more pleasant way of passing the remaining time during the drive home.

CHAPTER FOUR

A few days later, Lydia waited impatiently for Samuel to arrive at the bakery for his weekly order. In between assisting customers, she kept glancing out the front window and hoping to see his buggy pulling to a stop on the street outside. But there was no sign of him.

If her aunt had been working with her, Lydia's preoccupation would not have escaped the older woman's notice. But Aunt Martha was feeling a bit under the weather, so Lydia's uncle was helping out at the bakery on his usual day off instead.

Around midmorning, the shop became so busy that Lydia didn't have a chance to look up for even a quick glance out the window. The sound of the bell hanging above the door jovially announced the arrival of another customer, drawing Lydia's gaze.

Samuel. At last.

He stood just inside the bakery, and all the noise and hustle and bustle around her suddenly became muted. Samuel's eyes met hers, and he offered her a warm smile. Her mouth curved in response.

Lydia forced her gaze away from him to quickly finish boxing up David Lantz's purchase, repeating his farewell by rote. She noticed David exchange a few words with Samuel on his way out the door.

It took several minutes for Lydia to work through serving the line of customers ahead of Samuel. She turned her attention back to him as he stepped up to the counter to place his usual order. She rang up his purchase before reaching for a bakery bag and filling it.

"Can you take a break and sit with me as I eat one of these treats," Samuel asked as she handed the brown paper bag to him.

She turned to her uncle, who had just replenished a tray of blueberry muffins. "Is it all right if I take my break now, *Onkel*?"

"*Ya*," he replied, dusting off his hands and moving to take her place at the counter to assist the next customer.

As she rounded the glass display case and walked with Samuel toward a table in the corner, Lydia wiped her hands on her apron.

"Are you going to have anything to eat?" Samuel asked.

She shook her head in reply. "I'm not feeling hungry at the moment."

The community meeting a few days before had sparked an idea in her, but she wanted to discuss it with Samuel to get his opinion. She knew that Samuel, like many others, still held reservations about her progressive views. But she hoped to win him over.

After much consideration, she concluded that a *shared project* between the Amish and *Englisch* might help the traditional and progressive factions in their community overcome their differences.

Lydia waited until she and Samuel were both seated at the table in the corner and he had started to eat his banana nut muffin before she spoke. "I've been thinking, and I believe that the conservatives in our *gmay* might be more open to embracing change if they could see that it's possible to work together with the *Englisch* toward a common goal."

Samuel paused from devouring his sweet

treat, his expression turning contemplative. "What did you have in mind?"

"I was thinking of holding a benefit auction to raise funds for a community center that would serve both the *Amisch* and *Englisch* and bring the two groups together."

Samuel stopped eating completely to give his full attention to their conversation. "How would you go about organizing such an event?"

Lydia leaned forward across the table, her enthusiasm carrying clearly in her voice. "First, I want to gather a committee, representatives from both the *Amisch* and *Englisch* communities. Together, we'll plan and coordinate the auction. It will be an opportunity to see the value and strength of both groups working side by side."

Samuel's brow furrowed. "I doubt Levi will be in favor of such a project, and he's not likely to forego voicing his objections. He'll see your actions as a threat to our way of life, just as he did with other attempts to make changes in our *gmay*."

Lydia's heart felt a bit deflated by Samuel's apparent criticism of her idea, but she refused to let it deter her. While she anticipated the possibility of resistance from conservative members, she'd hoped for a more positive response from Samuel. She wondered if the still fragile bond they'd begun to re-forge since her return to town was strong enough to weather their differences.

"Do you feel the same way as Levi?" she asked, searching Samuel's gaze.

"*Nee*," Samuel answered.

He did, however, worry that Levi might try to cause problems—as he had in the past.

But unlike his brother, Samuel did not believe that working together with others who held differing views was a threat to his own traditions.

Was it truly possible for the Amish and *Englisch* communities to live in harmony with each other? It seemed too much to hope for given that the Amish community was divided against itself with conservative and progressive members unable to live in peaceful accord.

Lydia shifted forward in her chair once more, her expression one of earnestness. "I know that the factions within our *gmay* seem to be at an impasse about our views on outside influences, but it's my hope that by working together with *Englischers*, we can prove there's a way for us to coexist, to find a compromise that will satisfy both sides and benefit everyone."

"Perhaps you're right, Lydia." Maybe it was

time for Samuel to reevaluate his own stance and consider a path that honored their heritage while embracing the potential of the future. He stared into Lydia's eyes, unwavering conviction reflected in her gaze. Her words resonated within him, stirring a mixture of emotions. But the strongest one was hope. "You have my support on this project. Just tell me how I can help."

Lydia's expression filled with gratitude as she reached across the table and laid her hand on his arm. "*Danki*, Samuel. Your support means much to me, and I appreciate your willingness to step in and help."

He offered her a piece of the banana nut muffin that had sat abandoned on the table during her pitch and his approval thereof, and she accepted it with a slight smile. She chewed slowly, seeming more focused on her thoughts than what she was eating.

"So, where do we start?" he prompted.

They spent the next few minutes discussing potential committee members. Lydia pulled a notepad from her apron pocket to make a list of individuals' names from both communities who were known for their open-mindedness and willingness to embrace change.

* * *

Later that day, after the evening chores were done, Samuel sat out on the back steps of his farmhouse, bundled in his coat and watching the sunset. The air was crisp with a sharp bite that warned winter was not far off.

Lydia's ideas had continued to occupy Samuel's mind since he left the bakery hours earlier. He couldn't help but admire her determination to better the lives of everyone in town. She embraced the potential that change could bring rather than viewing it with fear.

She possessed a strength of conviction that was both inspiring and unsettling to Samuel. Her unwavering belief in the good that could come from building a bridge between the Amish and *Englisch* communities challenged his own long-held views.

He was determined to open his heart to the possibilities that lay ahead in the future —especially the possibility of what might be achieved by working together.

Long after the last bright blaze of colors had faded from the sky, Samuel finally stood up and went inside.

※ ※ ※

Over the next several days, when Lydia was not working in the bakery, she sought out those on her list, both Amish and *Englisch*, detailing her plan and inviting them to be part of the committee. She was appreciative that many responded with enthusiasm, intrigued by the prospect of collaboration.

Since Samuel had chores on the farm to see to and usually came into town only once or twice a week, he did not accompany her on this task. But she knew that the absence of his presence at her side was not an indication of his lack of support.

On the day the committee met for the first time, Samuel was among the group gathered at the Lapps' bakery after it closed for the day.

He sat in the chair next to Lydia, so close that his shoulder occasionally brushed against hers.

"I appreciate you all agreeing to join us here today," Lydia began. "I want to arrange something that will not only benefit our communities but also strengthen the bonds between us. With your help, I'd like to organize a benefit auction to raise funds to build a shared community center that will be open to all, a symbol of our willingness to embrace change and work together to build a better future."

Her words were met with nods of agreement and murmurs of support. Samuel glanced at Lydia, offering her an encouraging smile.

The next hour was filled with much discussion as various committee members shared their ideas. By the end of the meeting, everyone had pledged their commitment to the project, leaving Lydia with a renewed sense of purpose and hope for the future.

As Lydia pondered the day's events that evening, she realized that the connection she felt with Samuel ran deeper than friendship. It was a bond grounded in respect, shared values, and an unwavering commitment to their community.

But, does he see me as anything more than a friend? she wondered.

CHAPTER FIVE

Lydia's determination to make the benefit auction a success knew no bounds. With the committee's support, she embarked on a mission the following week to reach out to businesses in the surrounding area, seeking contributions and donations for the event. She believed that by involving the *Englisch* community and showcasing the generosity of both sides, they could foster a greater sense of unity.

Her aunt and uncle were the first people she approached to ask for a donation for the auction. Of course, they agreed and pledged to give several baskets of baked goods.

Lydia was pleased to be off to such a good start. However, her efforts at her next few stops at local Amish businesses were met with mixed responses. Some were receptive, while others remained skeptical, wary of the potential consequences of further outside influence. But Lydia pressed on, undeterred.

Opening the door to Mr. Troyer's buggy shop, where the scents of wood, leather, and axle grease mingled in the air, she was immediately greeted by the older man. He set down his tools and abandoned the repair he had been working on to approach her.

"How can I help you today, Lydia?" he asked as he wiped his hands on a rag.

"I was hoping that you might be able to donate an item or service to the auction I'm helping to organize to raise funds for the creation of a community center that will be shared by both the *Amisch* and *Englisch* residents in town," she explained, her eyes scanning the buggies lined up in various stages of construction.

Although Mr. Troyer's shop was known for its craftsmanship and dedication to preserving Amish traditions, his personal views leaned more toward the progressive. She was certain that he'd see the benefit in working together for a shared goal.

"That sounds like a very worthwhile cause." He tucked the worn rag into the pocket of his trousers. "I'd be happy to lend my support by donating a voucher for free repairs to a buggy."

"*Danki*, Mr. Troyer."

Lydia exited the shop to a sky covered with gray clouds threatening snow, so she decided to head home for the day. But as soon as she finished her work at the bakery the next day, she intended to resume her search for more donations.

The next afternoon, Samuel arrived unexpectedly at the bakery near the end of Lydia's shift.

"What are you doing here?" she asked, the words popping out of her mouth without any thought for how they might be interpreted.

"Aren't you happy to see me?" he asked in a teasing tone.

"*Ach*, of course," she replied quickly. Which was entirely true. His sudden appearance was a surprise but not an unpleasant one. "I just meant that it's not Friday, when you always come in for your usual order."

"I thought I'd join you today in collecting donations. If that's all right with you?"

Her non-verbal response was a broad smile that stretched across her entire face. "I'd be very pleased to have your company."

A short time later, they left the bakery

together, bundled up in warm coats and scarves against the cold temperature outside.

Snow and slush from the previous night's storm had been shoveled to the edges of the sidewalk, but the sun caused a considerable amount of melting, and the concrete was wet beneath their feet as they started walking along the main street of town.

"Where to first?" Samuel asked, tucking his gloved hands into his trouser pockets.

"I've already visited a number of *Amisch* businesses." Lydia named the people she'd spoken to the previous day. "But I'd like to continue stopping in to see more *Amisch* individuals today."

"What about *Englisch* businesses?" Samuel asked.

"I plan to start approaching them after I work through my list of potential *Amisch* donors. Let's head to Ruth Fisher's art gallery next."

Samuel nodded in agreement.

As they entered the storefront where Ruth displayed her artwork, Lydia's eyes were immediately drawn to the colorful nature paintings and landscapes hanging on the walls.

Ruth was a talented Amish artist who inherited the local gallery from an *Englisch* friend,

Adeline McCarthy, after she had been killed in a car accident six months prior.

Lydia had not yet been in town then, of course, but she learned of the details from her aunt.

Ruth appeared from the doorway located on the back wall and greeted them with a warm smile. Her hands and clothes were spotted with dots of paint, indicating they'd caught her in the middle of working on a project in her art studio in the back room.

"What brings you two here today?" she asked cheerily.

Lydia repeated the same request that she had made to Mr. Troyer and several others already.

Before Ruth could respond, the door from the street opened and David Lantz walked in.

Ruth's eyes brightened at the sight of him. After the courting couple exchanged a greeting, Ruth turned back to Lydia and Samuel.

"I could contribute a painting or a series of art classes to the auction. Or perhaps both."

"That's a *wunderbaar* idea," Lydia agreed, thinking it would provide an opportunity for the *Englisch* community to learn more about the Amish way of life through art.

"What are you talking about?" David

interjected.

Ruth quickly explained.

David's gaze shifted to Lydia. He seemed intrigued by the topic of their conversation, judging by his expression. "Where are you intending to hold this auction?"

Lydia was momentarily at a loss for words, realizing that she had not thought that far ahead. If they already had a community center, it would be the perfect place to hold the auction. But then, if it already existed, they wouldn't need to raise funds for its creation.

"The location of the auction hasn't been decided yet," Samuel answered on Lydia's behalf.

"If you're open to suggestions…" When David paused, Lydia indicated her assent with a nod, and he continued. "I've bought some land on the edge of town to build a house. There's a barn on the property. It's in rough shape, but it could be fixed up."

"I'm willing to help with that," Samuel volunteered. "And I'm sure others will be, too."

Lydia was grateful for the generosity displayed by so many local people. "*Danki*, David. And *danki*, Ruth, for your donation," she added.

After promising to talk again soon to hammer

out all the details, Lydia and Samuel excused themselves to continue their solicitations for more charitable contributions.

The ensuing days were a whirlwind of activity. Initially, when Lydia and Samuel began visiting *Englisch* businesses, the owners met their requests with skepticism. But Lydia's persuasive arguments soon won them over.

The response from the community was overwhelming, and donations began to pour in, which they stored in the back room of the bakery.

Some of the donations from the Amish would by nature only be bid on by other Amish, like Mr. Troyer's free buggy repairs. Likewise, some items and services donated by *Englisch* businesses would only be bid on by other *Englischers*.

But there were other things—such as the baskets of treats from the bakery, Ruth's art and painting lessons, and canned food from the local supermarket that was part of a national chain—that would likely draw bids from both Amish and *Englischers* in attendance at the auction.

Lydia was filled with a sense of accomplishment as she stood among the boxes of donated items, each one signifying the willingness of both the Amish and *Englisch* communities to come together for a good cause. The auction had transformed into something far greater than just that, though. It was a symbol of hope for the future.

As Lydia perused the various donations, she recognized that they represented more than their material value. They represented the possibilities that emerged when people set aside their differences in pursuit of a joint effort that would benefit many.

※ ※ ※

Samuel was amazed by Lydia's unwavering determination and her ability to inspire others and bring people together. He had a great deal of admiration for her, and their time spent working together had drawn the two of them closer than ever.

As the plans progressed for the charity auction, he found himself more and more invested in making it a success, and fixing up David Lantz's barn was the next step in preparing for the event.

Samuel met David on his property to assess the extent of the repairs needed to restore the dilapidated barn. They discussed the necessary materials and estimated how long the project would take to complete.

David's experience working in the *Englisch* world had given him valuable construction knowledge and skills, but Samuel was more than up to the task of making a significant contribution, too—even if it was only by providing another set of hands.

After they left the barn, David pointed out where he intended to build the house that he envisioned he and Ruth would live in together one day.

Samuel took heart in the living testimony that a person could return to the community and find contentment even after experiencing a much more modern life for several years.

Over the past few weeks, the fear that Lydia might decide to leave—just as Ruth's older sister, Hannah, did—had lingered in the back of Samuel's mind though he did not consciously acknowledge it until he stood on David's property. But as he chatted with David, he felt that fear disappear, much like a wave on the seashore obliterates ruts or grooves in the sand and makes it smooth and new.

Samuel couldn't ignore the undeniable

connection he felt with Lydia, the way being in her company brought him peace and their friendship, a newfound sense of purpose. He realized that, understandably, he had allowed his past disappointment with Hannah to color his perception. By holding on to the hurt in his past, he had been denying himself the chance to find happiness and love once more. But he was considering the possibility of a new path going forward.

When he was with Lydia, he couldn't help picturing a future with her. He just needed the courage to allow it to become more than the two of them working together as friends.

❈ ❈ ❈

The next weekend, more than half a dozen men arrived to help Samuel and David begin fixing up the barn for the auction, including Hannah and Ruth Fisher's father and younger brother and Mr. Troyer.

The sounds of sawing and hammering soon reverberated through the air, and the scent of freshly cut wood pleasantly permeated Samuel's nose.

The job was estimated to take a number of days to complete, but already, many members of the community had rallied together to help. However, for Samuel, one person's glaringly obvious absence cast a dark shadow over the day. Even though it came as no surprise, his brother's refusal to take part in the project still perturbed Samuel.

Levi remained steadfast in his opposition to change in their community, his disapproval of Lydia's actions growing more apparent with each passing day as he constantly criticized her intentions. He confronted Samuel several times about how he was aiding her efforts.

But when Samuel made it plain that he was not willing to stop working with her, Levi had begun treating Samuel with sullen silences or leaving a room as soon as Samuel entered.

Samuel knew that Levi's hostility stemmed from his frustration that not everyone agreed with his point of view. But it was naïve and unrealistic to expect everyone to think exactly the same way he did.

Samuel had realized that his own initial skepticism of Lydia's ideas was rooted in the fear of losing the traditional way of life that he cherished.

Then Lydia began to show him that progress and tradition could coexist.

Yet, try as he might, Samuel had not been able to convince his brother of that fact.

CHAPTER SIX

On Saturday morning, Lydia was filled with excitement as she headed to David Lantz's land, where the repairs to the barn were underway. Her uncle sat beside her driving the buggy while Lydia held a basket in her lap filled with treats from the bakery for the workers.

As they drew near, she could discern the rhythmic sound of hammers striking nails, which grew exponentially louder with their approach and arrival. The sight before her brought a smile to her face: a group of men, including Samuel, David, and other willing volunteers, working industriously to restore the barn. The noticeable improvements that had already been made were a testament to their collective efforts.

Uncle Henry drew the horse to a halt near the site, and Lydia climbed down from the buggy.

Their arrival had caught the attention of several people, and she called out a cheerful greeting.

Samuel set aside his hammer, wiped his perspiring forehead with his sleeve, and came to meet her, a warm smile on his face. Uncle Henry moved to talk to some of the other men, leaving Lydia and Samuel standing slightly apart from everyone else.

"It looks like you're making good progress," she remarked encouragingly.

Samuel nodded in agreement. "*Ya*, the barn will be ready for the auction in no time."

"That's *wunderbaar*." Lydia felt a rush of gratitude and admiration for the dedication of Samuel and the other men who had shown up to volunteer their time and assistance.

The fact that they were there proved that they believed in the cause. The atmosphere was filled with camaraderie and a shared purpose.

"Uncle Henry came to lend a hand," Lydia said, then lifted the basket she held in her hands, drawing Samuel's attention to it. "And I thought everyone here deserved a reward for their efforts."

She reached into the basket and pulled out a plastic-wrapped pastry that had been freshly baked that morning in the bakery's oven. Samuel accepted the offering from her gratefully, then accompanied her as she passed out delicious baked goods to the rest of the men.

Their expressions lit up with pleasure at the sight of the treats, and they took a break from their work to enjoy the delicacies after thanking Lydia for her thoughtfulness in providing them with refreshments.

Over the course of the following week, Lydia continued to secure more donations for the auction. And several customers at the bakery expressed curiosity and interest as they saw the positive impact of Lydia's efforts.

With each additional donation, her determination grew stronger, and soon the support from the community began to outweigh the resistance.

Her vision of a community center that would serve both the Amish and *Englisch* residents of the town was becoming more tangible with each passing day.

As the work on the barn neared completion, Lydia felt a sense of accomplishment and anticipation. They would soon be ready to hold the auction.

The only thing casting a slight shadow on her

joy was the fact that some conservative members of the community still had doubts about the endeavor and refused to support the auction—including Levi, Samuel's younger brother. He made no secret of the fact that he resented the changes she was trying to bring and the potential impact they could have on their community.

Others also shared his views and would not easily accept change, either, but Lydia was determined to stay the course, knowing that her efforts would benefit everyone.

❈ ❈ ❈

As the date of the auction drew closer, Lydia and other members of the committee that consisted of both the Amish and *Englischers* worked tirelessly to ensure that the event would be a success.

At last, the day of the auction arrived. People from both communities gathered in optimism and excitement. Laughter and friendly chatter filled the barn, erasing the boundaries that had once separated them.

The donations demonstrated the generosity and support of businesses and individuals from both the Amish and *Englisch*. One by one, items were showcased on the make-shift stage and auctioned off. The bidding was loud and enthusiastic.

Lydia found herself caught up in the fervor, her gaze darting from one bidder to another. But it wasn't just the riveting bids that held her attention. It was the sight of the two groups mingling together without the barriers that had once divided them, their differences seemingly having faded into insignificance as they united for a common purpose. Lydia was overwhelmingly grateful to witness the display of true harmony between two worlds that had often clashed.

The auction is turning out to be even more successful than I imagined!

Samuel, standing beside her, spoke softly in her ear. "You were right about *Amisch* and *Englischers* working together for a noble purpose, Lydia. You've shown us all what is possible when we set aside our differences and embrace change. You should be proud of what you've accomplished."

"What *we've* accomplished," she corrected. "I couldn't have done this without you and countless others. It's the result of the collective efforts of many people. I'm proud of all of us."

He reached out and took hold of her hand, squeezing it encouragingly in wordless agreement.

Lydia's heart swelled with elation, realizing that her efforts had not only brought the two communities together but also brought her and Samuel closer. Intertwining her fingers with his, they shared a silent understanding that the bond they formed as children had been strengthened over the past few weeks.

As the auction came to a close, Lydia was astonished at the record amount of money that had been raised in support of the cause to build a community center. It surpassed everyone's expectations, including her own.

There would still be challenges ahead, though. Not everyone would be in favor of more changes—even those that turned out to be good ones as the charity auction had proved to be.

❋ ❋ ❋

Samuel had watched with awe and not a small amount of pride as Lydia's vision unfolded before his eyes. Her unwavering commitment to fostering cooperation and understanding had brought about something extraordinary.

It was clear that the Amish and *Englisch* could indeed work together and bridge the gap that divided them for so long. But would the conservative and progressive factions within the Amish community ever be able to accomplish a similar feat? Samuel couldn't deny the doubts that filled his mind at the thought.

When he voiced the question to Lydia, however, her answer was filled with certainty. "Change doesn't mean we have to abandon our traditions. It means finding a way to adapt and grow while remaining true to our elemental values. It's about building bridges rather than walls."

Samuel took a moment to absorb her words deep into his soul, like a sponge increasing its capacity to retain water when completely submerged. His eyes were opened to the fact that Lydia's progressive ideas weren't about discarding their heritage. Instead, her belief was in embracing the possibilities of what could be while still maintaining the true essence of what it meant to be Amish.

As they stood there in the barn, surrounded

by the lingering atmosphere of accomplishment and success that had been created by the auction, Samuel made a silent promise to himself to be more open to embracing the changes that came their way and to support Lydia in her quest for a more connected community. She changed his perspective on so much, and he suddenly became aware just how strong his feelings for her had become in such a short time.

Lydia's plan to bring the Amish and *Englisch* together had garnered mixed reactions among the Amish, and tensions within the community were rising.

Adding to it was the ongoing conflict surrounding the proposed factory that an *Englisch* company planned to build in town. Ever since the idea was first introduced, the conservative and progressive factions had been divided, with some seeing it as an opportunity for jobs and increased prosperity, while others feared it would bring unwanted changes to their way of life.

Samuel felt caught in the middle, torn between his growing realization of the benefits the factory could offer to them and the knowledge that such a stance would put him at further odds with his brother.

As Samuel returned home later that day, he could already feel the tension in the air inside the farmhouse. When he walked into the kitchen, Levi was sitting at the table.

His brow was furrowed, and his expression exuded disapproval. "I see you're back," he stated theatrically, his tone curt.

But Samuel found that he preferred this surly response over his brother's recent stony silences. Nothing could be resolved between them when Levi was unwilling to talk to Samuel about the issue.

Perhaps nothing could be resolved, though.

They would never see eye to eye on the subject of the auction, which Levi hadn't even bothered to ask after. And it was no secret that the younger man was staunchly opposed to the factory, viewing it as a threat to their traditional way of life.

Samuel filled a glass with water at the sink and carried it to the table. Pulling out a chair, he sat down. Even though he knew it would likely cause an argument, he couldn't help telling Levi about the success of the auction.

Levi, rather than taking at least some interest in his brother's life and displaying any form of positive reaction, scoffed in response. "Has Lydia brainwashed you now?"

"*Nee*. Her ideas don't throw the baby out with the bathwater; she looks for ways to embrace progress where it aids people but doesn't forsake her roots. Her ideas have brought about *gut* for our *gmay*—"

"Next, you'll be telling me that you support the factory, too."

Samuel didn't reply since he was still undecided on the matter.

Levi took his silence as tacit agreement and glared at him. "How can you ignore the harm that will most certainly be unleashed from such an encroachment of the *Englisch* world on our *gmay*?"

Samuel took a deep breath, forcing himself to remain patient and polite in the face of his brother's anger. "Did you ever stop to consider that we could maybe find a way to preserve our traditions while also embracing progress?"

Levi's mouth tightened in derision, his eyes narrowing. "*Progress*? Is that what you call it? Well, I call it a betrayal of our values, Samuel. We've managed just fine without the influence of the *Englisch* world. We don't need their factories and their modern ways."

Despite his effort to remain calm, Samuel's frustration began to mount at Levi's unwillingness to even consider a different perspective. He took a drink of water in a bid to manage his temper. "Levi, I respect your opinion, but I believe there's room for compromise. We can find a balance between preserving our traditions and embracing opportunities for the future of our *gmay*."

"Compromise?" Levi spat. "This isn't a matter of compromise, Samuel." He slammed his hand on the table in his vehemence, causing Samuel to jerk back in response. In his heightened state of dogmatism, Levi didn't seem to notice and continued, "This is a matter of standing firm in our beliefs. If we don't remain separate from the *Englisch*, they'll corrupt our way of life."

Samuel's patience was wearing precariously thin, but he knew he had to keep calm at all costs. He couldn't allow the disagreement with his brother to tear their relationship apart. "Levi, change is inevitable," he replied, unintentionally echoing the words Lydia had said to him.

Levi abruptly pushed his chair back and stood, his face fiery red with anger. "*You've* changed, Samuel. Ever since Lydia came back to town, you've allowed her to indoctrinate you with her progressive ideas."

Samuel watched open-mouthed in bewilderment as Levi stormed out of the kitchen, leaving him alone with the weight of their argument hanging thickly in the air. He sighed, realizing that finding common ground with his brother wouldn't be easy.

But he couldn't ignore the growing conviction within him that they could benefit from being open to new ideas rather than blanketly opposing any sort of change—viewing all change as injurious regardless of whether some might actually be good for the community.

The next day, as Samuel tried to focus on farm chores, the strain between him and Levi remained palpable. Every interaction was filled with icy glares and terse exchanges from his sibling. It was clear that from Levi's perspective, their differing views on the factory had driven a wedge between them.

Finally, unable to stand the awkward tension any longer, Samuel determined that they would both benefit from a respite from each other and sought out tasks that he could see to on his own.

While repairing a leather harness in the barn, his thoughts drifted to Lydia. His growing relationship with her was at the root of the current contention between him and Levi, but he wasn't prepared to stop spending time with her, not even to make peace with his brother. Yet, he needed to find some way to compromise with Levi, to mend the rift that had formed between them.

At that moment, Samuel made a decision: he couldn't let the disagreement with Levi jeopardize his bond with Lydia. He wasn't sure just how exactly to remove the wedge between himself and Levi, but he felt a renewed sense of resolve. As the sun began to set, Samuel returned to the farmhouse, determined to try again to get through to his brother.

CHAPTER SEVEN

Lydia stood at the front window of the bakery in the predawn darkness before the shop opened, looking out at the main street of town. Any minute, she would go help her aunt finish baking in the back room, but just for a moment, she lingered by the window, lost in thought.

A sigh escaped her lips, the division within the community weighing heavily on her heart. She knew that finding a way to bridge the gap between the two sides and reach a compromise would be difficult. Her mind wandered to Samuel. When he had come into the bakery the previous week to pick up his usual order, she saw the struggle in his eyes, torn between his loyalty to his brother's unbending insistence on maintaining the old traditions and his own growing inclination to see things from Lydia's and others' more progressive point of view and to realize the value in such a perspective.

She sensed his genuine desire to do what was best for the community even as his attempts at trying to make amends with his brother were thwarted at every turn.

Lydia had spent countless hours contemplating how to unite the two factions—not just Samuel and Levi but all the conservative and progressive members of the community. In order to find common ground amidst their differences, she concluded that she needed to find a way to foster empathy and understanding. She knew it wouldn't be easy to effect such change after years of people becoming firmly entrenched in their positions on opposite sides of the divide, and fear of the unknown often clouded judgment. But she refused to let that stand in the way of the possibility for their community to mend the breach at its heart by seeking the means to live in harmony.

Over the course of the next few days, Lydia began to speak with customers in the bakery, engaging them in conversation about any concerns and fears they might have regarding the proposed factory and acknowledging the validity of their perspectives. Each afternoon, after she was finished with her work, she made her way around town, approaching other members of the community to listen to their thoughts on the matter, too.

At first, she was nervous about broaching the topic that had caused so much tension. But as the discussions progressed, she shared more and more of her own vision of what was possible by being open to change. Forging a path that honored their past but also looked forward to the future. She described a town that thrived while still staying rooted in its traditions. A place where the Amish and *Englisch* could coexist and learn from one another.

Lydia witnessed the capacity for change in Samuel—how he embraced new ideas without losing sight of the values that defined them as Amish—and she hoped that others would follow his lead. She respected his willingness to listen to different perspectives and consider the potential benefits of the factory, which she knew had not been an easy decision for him. His internal struggle, a necessary part of his journey, had been visible in his eyes as he began to question his previous way of thinking.

The conflict within the community underscored how hard it was for people to leave the familiar and step into the unknown. It was not surprising that so many fought against it.

Lydia wasn't sure if she would be able to change any hearts or minds with her campaign of encouraging others to be more accepting of progress, but the mere fact that she was taking some sort of action made her feel as though she was making at least a modicum of difference.

Uncle Henry praised her efforts after overhearing one of her conversations with a customer at the bakery. "You speak with such conviction, Lydia. Your words resonate with people, and I believe there are a number of them who are now questioning their formerly unyielding resistance."

"I hope you're right," she replied.

But despite her uncertainty, her uncle's heartening words buoyed her spirits.

Lydia felt a renewed sense of purpose and validation that her efforts to bridge the divide and find a compromise were not in vain despite whatever obstacles might still lie ahead on the path to change. With determination, the hurdles along the way could be overcome—to lead the community toward a better future.

※ ※ ※

In the days that followed, Lydia formed a committee to facilitate a new goal—to work with the *Englisch* developer of the proposed factory to ensure that the construction process would still respect the values and traditions of the Amish.

Unlike the committee for the charity auction, this one comprised only of Amish—apart from the *Englisch* developer with whom they would meet at a later stage—as Lydia believed it to be the best way of ensuring that conservative members would not be immediately set against the committee because they were suspicious of its motives.

Samuel was the first person she asked to join, and he agreed without hesitation. She also approached David Lantz and Ruth Fisher, Mr. Troyer, and half a dozen others. Some of them had been on the auction committee together, but she made a specific effort to invite other people to take part in the group as well. The committee, although consisting of members of both progressive and conservative leanings, had commonality in that they were individuals who Lydia believed were dedicated to finding a compromise that would benefit everyone.

A week later, the Lapps' bakery again became a gathering place for the new committee's first meeting. The assembled members sat at the tables scattered around the front of the shop.

Seated next to Samuel, Lydia perused the room, her gaze settling briefly on each committee member in acknowledgment. "*Danki* for coming here today. I appreciate your willingness to work together and find a solution to the opposing views about the proposed *Englisch* construction project in town."

Mr. Troyer shifted in his seat at another table, saying, "The factory has the potential to bring growth and opportunities. But it's important that we ensure it aligns with our values."

David nodded in agreement. "I've seen firsthand how factories can disrupt communities, but I've also seen the benefits they can bring. We need to find a way to mitigate any negative impacts as the construction moves forward."

Ruth, who was sitting beside David, chimed in next. "I believe art can be a bridge between our communities. Local *Amisch* artwork could be incorporated into the design of the factory, creating a space that reflects our heritage and traditions."

"What about making sure that the construction is done with respect for the environment and our land?" asked an older man, a conservative farmer who lived near the proposed factory site.

"Sustainable materials could be used to build the factory, along with a traditional design that blends in with its surroundings," David replied, offering expertise and knowledge he'd gained from his time working in construction in the *Englisch* world.

Hope ballooned in Lydia as she listened to committee members exchanging constructive dialogue. They were united in their desire to find a compromise.

But she also knew that the greatest challenge was still ahead— Levi's conservative group, the most vocal and hostile opponents of the factory who saw Lydia's efforts as a threat to their way of life. She refused to allow that to stop her, though.

※ ※ ※

At the start of the new year a few weeks later,

David and other committee members scheduled a meeting with the developer to discuss their issues and try to negotiate a plan going forward. They needed to navigate complex deliberations about zoning regulations and environmental impact while advocating for the Amish community's needs.

As news of the committee's efforts spread throughout town, tensions rose and confrontations broke out between individuals more often, leaving Samuel feeling increasingly anxious.

His participation on the committee antagonized Levi as expected—and set back any tenuous ground Samuel had gained in his attempted reconciliation with his brother. They had put their differences aside to celebrate Christmas together, but their truce didn't last beyond the season of peace and goodwill to all men. Nor did it make his brother look any more charitably on Samuel's association with Lydia.

Levi and his followers saw Lydia as an instigator-disruptor, someone who was betraying their traditions and trying to force unwanted changes in their *gmay*. They continued to oppose the factory, believing that it would bring an influx of *Englisch* influence that would erode their way of life.

Samuel tried to shield Lydia from Levi's hostility as best he could, worrying that his brother's group might resort to harassing her at the bakery or that another unfortunate incident would occur, like when the Fishers' barn was deliberately set on fire.

The arson was believed to have occurred because Ruth and her elder sister, Hannah, befriended Adeline McCarthy, the *Englisch* artist who had lived in town before she died in a car accident. However, officially, the motive behind the fire remained unestablished because the authorities had never been able to prove who was responsible for the malicious act.

When Samuel made his weekly trip to the bakery that Friday, he asked Lydia if she could take a break and sit with him.

"*Ya*," she instantly agreed.

Once they were settled at the table, Samuel extended his hand and she instinctively reached out to clasp it.

"How are you, Lydia?" he asked. "Levi and his friends haven't been bothering you, have they?" He tightened his hold on her hand and didn't relax his grip until she shook her head in denial. "That's *gut*."

But Samuel feared the situation was likely to worsen in the coming weeks and months as the plans for the construction of the factory moved ahead. His heart felt burdened and weighed down by the resistance he and Lydia were facing in their joint endeavor—and their growing relationship with each other.

She squeezed his hand as though sensing his thoughts and wanting to offer him comfort. "Things will work out," she assured him.

Her words didn't comfort him, however. A deep sigh escaped from his tight chest. "I want to believe that, Lydia, but it's difficult. Levi and his group are so set in their ways that they see any change as a threat."

"We must trust in *Gott* and the strength of our *gmay*. We've come this far already. We can't allow fear to stand in our way and stop us from continuing to push forward."

Samuel knew she was right, but it did little to alleviate his worry and doubts.

He glanced away from Lydia for a moment and was surprised to see Hannah Fisher at the bakery counter being attended to by Mrs. Lapp.

Beneath his gaze, Hannah turned with a brown paper bag in hand and started walking toward the shop door. Her steps paused as she spotted Samuel at the corner table, but when she noticed Lydia sitting with him, Hannah gave him a small wave, then continued on her way to the door without going over to greet him. She was gone from the bakery in a matter of seconds—before Samuel could say a word or decide what, if anything, he wanted to do.

He wasn't familiar with the strange emotions that coiled in his belly at seeing Hannah again. But thoughts of her were swiftly pushed from his mind as Lydia's voice drew his attention and more pressing concerns took precedence.

CHAPTER EIGHT

Hannah Fisher walked away from the Lapps' bakery, pulling her coat tighter around herself to ward off the early January frigid temperature. She was home visiting her family during her college winter break but would be leaving town again soon since the holidays had passed and classes would be resuming.

Her younger sister, Ruth, had told her about the success of a charity auction that the Amish and *Englisch* worked together in organizing and conducting. Hannah was pleased, but she hadn't seen the news as quite as big a cause for celebration as Ruth since it was only the more progressive members of the Amish community who supported working with the *Englischers* on the auction.

The conservative faction remained unyielding

in their advocation to maintain their traditions and resist change, which meant that any attempts at progress within the Amish community were still met with opposition, as had been proven by the widening rift caused by the proposed factory on land owned by an *Englisch* company. The two sides remained unequivocally divided.

Hannah felt disheartened by the conflict within the community seemingly to have grown even more contentious than when she was last there the previous summer. Prior to returning to school in the fall, her own efforts to bring changes to the community had failed dismally.

After witnessing that the situation had only worsened since then, Hannah had little hope of things improving any time soon, if ever. Over the past few months, she had been toying with pursuing a career outside the Amish community, and she found herself leaning even further in that direction.

Her thoughts shifted back to her brief encounter with Samuel in the bakery a few minutes before. She had discerned the closeness between him and Lydia Lapp as they sat together and didn't want to intrude on the couple.

It seems I lost my chance with Samuel. He's moved

on.

Hannah wasn't quite sure how she felt about that. Granted, she had wanted to attend college and chose it over marrying him, yet, it still came as a shock to see that he'd moved on.

Surely, she hadn't expected him to wait for her indefinitely. But perhaps subconsciously she imagined that they might pick up where they'd left off if she decided to return to a traditional life after exploring the outside world.

Shame washed over Hannah for viewing Samuel as someone to fall back on if she changed her mind when she had been unwilling to make any sort of commitment to him that would have given him a reason to hold onto hope while she was away. Even though she had considered him her fallback, she did so unintentionally. Still, it wasn't fair to him. And admittedly, her heart was not broken by his expedient moving on.

The reason became crystal clear to Hannah: she didn't love Samuel as anything more than a friend. And as his friend, she didn't begrudge him a chance to find happiness. It didn't change the fact that she wasn't sure she fit in there anymore, though. Maybe it would never be her home again and she would only ever return to town for brief visits.

※ ※ ※

Samuel barely had a chance to exchange more than a few words with Hannah while she was in town before she was gone again. As he reflected, he realized that seeing her again didn't cause as much pain as he had imagined it might. Perhaps it was because his mind was completely consumed with the ongoing conflict within his community. Or maybe it was because he had finally moved on. Or both.

He knew that Lydia had played a large part in opening his heart. He had let her in, and the more time he spent with her, the deeper his feelings for her grew. He felt much more for her than mere friendship.

As he headed to the barn to tend the animals, his thoughts turned once more to brainstorm a way to resolve the impasse between the conservative and progressive factions. It had been a challenging few weeks. The proposed factory had stirred up a whirlwind of emotions within the community, dividing neighbors and friends. And Samuel was caught in the middle.

Levi and his group vigorously opposed the unwanted changes the factory would bring to their town. Samuel understood their concerns, and at times he could almost give in to being swept away by the same fears himself. But then he would remember Lydia's rational reasoning; he couldn't ignore the possibilities that the factory presented—a chance for progress, employment, and prosperity for the community.

Conflicting thoughts bounced around Samuel's mind like rubber balls, bumping into and ricocheting off of each other. He needed to talk about things to stop the bouncing balls and make sense of them, but the one person with whom he used to be able to talk about his troubles—his younger brother—was no longer someone in whom Samuel could confide and share his worries.

But there was still someone he could confide in. Lydia.

She reminded Samuel of someone determinedly persevering to finish an obstacle course race, going around, over, under, through whatever blocked their path, even if it slowed progress significantly, so long as they were still making forward progress. She had already succeeded in building a bridge between the Amish and *Englisch*. And her efforts to find a compromise between the opposing factions within the Amish community was gaining momentum with some of the conservative members, such as the individuals who had agreed to join the committee to discuss the factory.

Lydia was a beacon of hope in such turbulent times, showing him that common ground could be found if people were willing to persevere. Her optimism and dedication were inspiring.

Something clicked into place, and Samuel realized he couldn't stay in a state of vacillation, holding onto his own doubts even while he aided Lydia in her causes—doubts he had refused to admit to himself still lingered in the back of his mind. He had to fully believe in their mission, just as Lydia did. He did not want any hesitation on his part to be the reason they didn't succeed in their goal.

Together, united, they could make a difference.

A swell of newfound resolve bubbled up in Samuel, and the bouncing balls in his mind lost momentum, slackening to a slow roll and coming to a state of inertia.

Starting the very next day, Samuel threw

himself wholeheartedly into Lydia's efforts. They worked side by side, reaching out to community members and seeking out ways to address the concerns of those who opposed the factory. He was grateful for the decline in farm work during the winter, as it allowed him to spend more time in town with Lydia without shirking his responsibilities at home.

Gradually, Samuel and Lydia's persistence paid off. As more individuals saw the positive impact of their efforts, resistance began to diminish. People started to listen, to see the potential for growth and harmony that the factory represented.

Over the next several months, the community meetings became more productive, with lively discussions and a genuine willingness by most in attendance to find common ground. There was still some opposition from the staunchest traditionalists who refused to consider any efforts to compromise, but things were starting to appear more positive than they had in a long time.

Samuel worked alongside Lydia, witnessing the transformation unfold before his eyes. It was a testament to the power of unity, the strength of their community, and the potency of prayer.

At the same time, Lydia continued to run with

her plans for the town's community center.

After raising a considerable amount of money for building the center, they needed to decide on a location. The committee considered finding a space to rent or a place that the owner would be willing to donate. But most committee members were in favor of constructing the building themselves on a plot of vacant land.

Of course, that would be more expensive than either of the other two options. But they could fashion the center exactly as they wanted it, and the cost would not be exorbitant if they could find people willing to donate most of the materials and labor.

Since that was not a given, Lydia put forward the idea to start planning a second fundraiser. But there was debate about whether it should be another auction or some other different type of event such as a craft fair.

Samuel's admiration, appreciation, and affection for Lydia grew as she continued to take on new projects to better the community. He saw her not only as a strong advocate for change but as a woman of unwavering determination and compassion. She had opened his eyes to the possibilities that lay beyond the boundaries of an unyielding adherence to tradition.

Samuel recognized that love for Lydia was blossoming within his heart, intertwining with his respect and appreciation for her. She had become more than just a friend and partner in their endeavors.

His desire for a more traditional life when it came to a wife and children remained unchanged, though. After the failure of his courtship with a progressive-minded woman who wanted more than to be merely a farmer's wife, he didn't want to make the same mistake again.

Is Lydia someone with whom I can settle down, share my life, and build a familye *that lives with a high view of our traditions?*

❊ ❊ ❊

The early spring day dawned with clear skies, and a gentle breeze blew across the main street of town as the residents went about their daily tasks. However, as the morning wore on, gloomy gray clouds began to roll in and obscured the sun. Talk of the approaching storm was the topic of almost every conversation that Lydia had with the customers at the bakery.

Outside, the wind picked up, kicking bits of trash out of its path like a petulant teenager and carrying an eerie sense of foreboding. The day darkened as ominous clouds covered the sky.

A deep sense of unease skittered through Lydia as she moved to look out the front window at the rapidly changing sky. Her hand flew to her throat and a gasp slipped from her lips as she spotted a gray funnel cloud descending over the hills to the west of town. Its massive form twisted and turned with deadly intent on destruction, nature's fury uncaring of what or who lay in its path.

Lydia's hands shot up to cover her mouth as the tornado stretched down to touch the innocent countryside. The rapidly spinning funnel raked across the land, tearing apart homes and flinging trees and vehicles as if they were nothing more than kids' toys.

"*Ach du Gott*," someone whispered in a horrified voice behind Lydia.

But she didn't turn to see who had spoken, unable to drag her gaze away from the disaster being waged on the town's outskirts. She could only watch helplessly, her chest constricting at the dreaded realization that there was nothing anyone could do to stop this destructive force of nature.

Will the tornado turn in this direction and destroy the entire town? Will any of us be spared?

Lydia began to pray to the only One who could save them.

The tornado stayed on its course, then veered away from them and disappeared back into the heavens. It had lasted only a few minutes, but the devastation left in its wake was enormous and extensive.

The businesses and homes in town had escaped unscathed, a small blessing amidst the chaos and desolation, but the farmhouses scattered across the countryside, where families had lived for generations, bore the brunt of nature's wrath.

Lydia's heart sank as she thought of the people who had just moments before called those wrecked and razed structures *home*. She imagined their fear and desperation as they clung to one another while the tornado ravaged their homes. She prayed that no lives were lost. Tears welled in her eyes at the thought. She hoped they had been able to find shelter in time.

But where will they go now that their homes are gone or uninhabitable?

Lydia's resolve suddenly reasserted itself

inside her. She might not have been able to stop the tornado, but there was something she could do to help those most severely affected by it. She knew that the true strength of their community would be tested in the face of such adversity.

With a deep breath, she stepped away from the window, ready to begin a relief effort by mobilizing the community to aid those in need.

The bakery door burst open, and Samuel rushed inside. His wild eyes scanned the room until he caught sight of Lydia. He was at her side in an instant and pulled her into a tight embrace. "*Danki* to *Gott* that you're all right, Lydia."

She drew comfort from the feel of his arms wrapped around her. "And you're okay, too."

"*Ya.*" He finally released her and stepped back. "I was driving into town when I saw the tornado."

Samuel's family farm was located east of town, so Lydia didn't have to ask if his home was still standing.

Unfortunately, there were many who had not been so lucky.

Yet, while lost loved ones could not be recovered, homesteads and structures could be rebuilt.

CHAPTER NINE

Lydia sat beside Samuel on his buggy seat as the two of them drove out to assess the devastation caused by the tornado. They were joined by David Lantz, whose construction expertise would be invaluable in their venture.

The once serene and peaceful countryside had been turned into a landscape of destruction. Trees had been uprooted, and debris lay scattered everywhere. The community Lydia loved had been shattered in an instant.

They reached the first farm that had been in the path of the tornado, and her eyes widened with disbelief as she surveyed the aftermath.

A pile of jagged chunks of wood and window frames with broken glass were all that were left where a home once stood. Cherished possessions were strewn around the yard, many of them damaged beyond repair.

Climbing down from the buggy, Lydia approached the shell-shocked family. Her heart ached at the sight of the tears running down the faces of the two children.

"Our home is gone," the smallest girl whimpered, clenching a tattered rag doll to her chest as her father held her in his arms.

He patted her back in an attempt to console her. His expression was stoic, but it was plain he was just as anxious and unsettled by what had happened.

"Where will we go now, *Maem*?" the older girl asked with a sniffle.

Her mother shook her head in uncertainty.

David stepped forward to provide an answer. "You can stay at the barn on my property that we used for the charity auction a few months ago. Any others who need a place to go are *willkumm* to shelter there, too."

Though worry still shadowed the woman's eyes, her expression turned grateful. "*Danki*, David."

A few hours later, as the sun began to set on the ravaged countryside, Lydia stood amid the ruins, her heart filled with sorrow. She knew that the road to recovery would be long and arduous, but she was confident that, together, they would rebuild the homes that had been lost and restore the community's sense of security.

They had weathered the storm—not just physically but emotionally as well—and Lydia was certain that they would emerge stronger and more united, ready to face any challenges that lay ahead.

She accompanied Samuel to the barn on David's property to see what help the two of them could offer at the temporary shelter for the families who had been left homeless. Samuel coordinated the placement of makeshift beds while Lydia distributed blankets. But she knew that the people would need so much more.

"These *familye* have lost everything," she said in a low voice to Samuel so that those nearby would not overhear her. "We must do whatever we can to provide them with food and clothing as well as shelter."

Samuel nodded, his eyes reflecting the same resolve. "You're right, Lydia. We'll seek out support from others in the *gmay*. We have to come together in this time of crisis."

Ruth Fisher, along with her mother and younger sister, arrived with a basket of sandwiches and pots of stew to feed everyone at the shelter that evening.

The next morning, Lydia and Samuel immediately started organizing a large-scale relief effort. Lydia reached out to local businesses and organizations, explaining the situation and requesting donations. Samuel took charge of coordinating the logistics, ensuring that the resources were delivered to the temporary shelter on David's property.

Over the course of the next few days, Lydia and Samuel worked together, receiving donations, sorting clothing, and preparing meals. The outpouring of aid from both Amish and *Englisch* sources was overwhelming, and Lydia felt a renewed sense of hope.

She'd witnessed the strength and resilience of the Amish community as they relied on their faith to see them through the difficult time and supported one another. Despite the tragedy, they'd rediscovered the power of unity and compassion. The tornado had tested their community, but it also revealed the true heart of the Amish in their willingness to help others.

In the days that followed, the Amish community rallied together, setting aside their differences to assist their neighbors. They worked tirelessly to clear debris, salvaging what they could, and offering comfort and support to those who had lost everything. Though the tornado had left a scar on the landscape, the bonds of friendship and kinship were strengthened as countless people lent a helping hand and provided a shoulder to lean on.

Through it all, Lydia and Samuel found solace in each other's presence. Their shared experiences deepened their connection, and they became a source of strength for one another. In the midst of the chaos, their bond had intensified.

Lydia was not naïve about the fact that their journey together was far from over; many obstacles were yet to come, but with their shared determination, they would overcome them.

※ ※ ※

Although the aftermath of the tornado had left Samuel's heart heavy, seeing the way the community came together in the face of adversity lifted the weight from his chest. The tornado had stripped away the superficial differences and divisions, leaving only the community's shared bond and faith in God.

Samuel found himself drawn to the makeshift shelter that had been set up in the barn to provide a temporary haven for those who lost their homes. The sight of families leaning on each other, finding solace and comfort together amidst the chaos, moved Samuel deeply.

Lydia stood at the center of the bustling activity. She turned to face him, and a gentle smile graced her lips.

He returned her smile as he approached her. "I don't want to interrupt your work."

"You're not interrupting," she assured him.

Whatever else he might have said remained unspoken as David came up beside them. "Samuel, I could use your help."

"Of course," he replied and followed the man out of the barn.

David requested that Samuel join the rebuilding efforts at the nearby farms, and Samuel nodded in agreement even though it would mean spending less time with Lydia.

❉ ❉ ❉

As the calendar page turned from April to

May and the earth burst forth with renewed life, the community slowly began to heal. Homes were rebuilt, and families were able to move out of the temporary shelter.

Samuel perceived that it wasn't merely the physical rebuilding of homes and farms that occurred over the recent weeks; a bridge between many members of the opposing factions of the Amish community had been formed as well.

He only wished that his brother was numbered among that group. While Levi did pitch in to build a new home for a neighbor, his rigid opposition to change had not been altered. Nor had his feelings toward Lydia softened.

As the properties that had be decimated by the tornado were reestablished and restored, the proposal for the factory reemerged as a source of contention, reigniting the tension that had divided the community just weeks before. The previous rift that cut its way back through the town was almost visible it was so pervasive, and it threatened to pull the conservative and progressive Amish apart again.

Discussions and debates turned into arguments, and tempers flared. In the bakery, Lydia watched as neighbors whispered to one another, brows furrowed with concern.

While the tornado brought everyone together with a common goal, it hadn't changed people's stances for or against the factory. Those in support of the development continued to argue that it would bring benefits to the town, such as jobs and economic prosperity, while others remained convinced that it would cause undesirable changes and threaten their way of life.

The weight of the disagreement hung heavy in the air, casting a cloud of uncertainty over everything. Finding a resolution wouldn't be easy, but Lydia was determined to bridge the divide and bring the community together once again. She believed in the potential of the factory to bring positive change without compromising their traditions. It was an uphill battle, but she was ready to face it head-on.

At the next community meeting, she was one of the first to speak up. "I understand the concerns that surround the proposal for the factory. The preservation of our way of life is just as important to me as it is to all of you. But we must also consider the potential benefits that this opportunity can give us."

Levi, seated with other members of his

conservative group, crossed his arms over his chest and scowled. "Lydia, we've heard your arguments before. Yet, we've seen the effects of progress on other communities. We won't let our traditions be compromised by the *Englisch* ways."

Those near him murmured in affirmation of his words.

Lydia met Levi's gaze with unwavering determination but forbearance and gentleness. "I respect your perspective, but we must also recognize that our *gmay* is evolving. Our youth seek opportunities beyond farming, and the factory could provide them with jobs close to home, allowing them to support their *familye* while still being a part of our *gmay*."

Levi's expression hardened as his eyes narrowed in distrust. "You may believe that, Lydia, but I see the dangers. Any outside influence is a threat to our way of life, and I won't stand idly by and watch as our traditions are snuffed out. The encroachment of the *Englisch* world will tempt the youth away from the simplicity of our faith."

Voices rose from the crowd, expressing agreement or dissent. The tension was unmistakable, the weight of the decision resting heavily on each individual's shoulders.

Samuel stood from his seat beside Lydia. "I believe that Lydia has a valid point that is worth pausing to consider. We can't dismiss this opportunity without bearing its potential benefits in mind. We've faced challenges before and found ways to adapt while preserving our values; this is not the first time we are assessing advancements and their impact on our way of life—and I assure you that it won't be the last. Imagine what our ancestors debated as each modern convenience was introduced to the *Englisch* world. We can follow their example: honor our roots, our traditions, and our faith while embracing the benefits that progress offers."

Lydia's heart swelled in gratitude for Samuel's support and solidarity. She knew it wasn't an easy act for him to openly oppose his brother before all that were gathered. She remembered his initial resistance to change and admired him for being open-minded enough to listen to a different perspective and see the value in it.

Samuel taking such a visible stand beside her stirred Lydia's hope that his feelings for her had grown just as strong as hers had become for him over the past few months as they worked together on various projects for the betterment of their community.

* * *

Samuel sat back down beside Lydia. The tension hung thick in the air. He glanced around, observing and interpreting the faces of his fellow community members, each holding their own stance on the matter. His heart ached as he saw the division among his people. He longed for unity, for a resolution that would honor both sides. He was almost afraid to meet his brother's eyes after stating his opposing opinion so blatantly, but he forced himself to look at Levi.

Anger was written in bold, caps, and italics on his brother's face as Levi glared at him. But Samuel wouldn't let that stop him from taking a stand in support of his reformed convictions. He respected his brother's right and desire to defend his own viewpoint, but how Levi went about trying to convince others to see things his way was likely to do more harm than good.

Levi and his conservative group were staunch traditionalists, determined to preserve the Amish way of life at all costs. And Samuel had been concerned by their methods more than once.

Hostile confrontations and intimidation tactics were not the way to try to get their point across to those who held different views from them.

In sharp contrast, Lydia's approach of openness and cooperation succeeded in changing many hearts and minds in the community.

Samuel had struggled to reconcile his loyalty to the traditions and values that shaped his life with the growing understanding of the possibilities that progress could offer. But seeing Lydia's unwavering dedication to finding a compromise that would satisfy both sides persuaded Samuel to support her.

He expected Levi to blast him with angry condemnation publicly in the middle of the community meeting. But his brother somehow found the restraint to wait until the two of them were alone in their buggy on the way home before he voiced his censure.

"Have you forsaken our way of life, Samuel? Have you forgotten the teachings that have guided us for generations?"

"I haven't forgotten," Samuel replied. "Nor do I intend to abandon our way of life. But I've come to realize that progress doesn't have to mean the loss of our values and traditions."

"Well, I don't agree. Any compromise is one we cannot afford to make. Not when it jeopardizes our way of life and spreads modern thinking to our *gmay* that sullies our separation from worldly ways and values. We must stand firm in maintaining the old ways."

The rest of the buggy drive to their farmhouse was completed in fraught silence, Samuel and Levi being stuck in a stalemate—as they had been for months.

When they arrived home, Samuel headed to the barn to finish a few chores. Even with all the projects he had joined Lydia in undertaking for the betterment of the community, he made sure to do his fair share of the chores on the farm, fully aware that if he started shirking his responsibilities, it would only compound Levi's resentment toward him. Samuel hated being at odds with his brother, but there just didn't seem to be any straightforward way to resolve their differing views.

CHAPTER TEN

Over the next two weeks, members of the community engaged in heated discussions debating the merits of the factory proposal. Lydia persevered in advocating for a compromise, urging the community to explore ways to ensure that their values and traditions would not be infringed upon by the *Englisch* development and that the factory would be built in a way that respected the Amish way of life. She listened to both sides' concerns and contentions, always searching for common ground and ways to address fears and reservations.

Slowly but surely, with Lydia playing mediator and humbly reiterating and validating each person's expressed perspective and concerns yet gently coaxing them to look at things from a different angle, to put themselves in the other side's shoes, a sense of identification and understanding emerged between many, and tensions began to ease slightly. This encouraged Lydia to keep working to bring the two sides together because her efforts *were* making a difference. She was certain that they could find a balance that accommodated the town's economic growth without sacrificing their cherished way of life.

The committee that Lydia had formed before the tornado resumed meeting with the developer. Their recommendations included provisions for reduced impact on the environment, limited working hours to respect the Amish Sabbath, and a commitment to preserve the agricultural land surrounding the factory.

At the next community meeting, David gave an update on how the collaboration and discussions were going.

"Things are looking promising," he said in conclusion.

"Let's take a vote to see how many are in favor of the factory now," Mr. Troyer suggested.

As a vote was cast, Lydia's heart pounded in anticipation. The outcome would determine their community's next step and direction, and the implications were significant.

When the votes were tallied, the result was almost evenly split, leaving the community in a state of impasse, with no clear resolution on the divide separating them.

Lydia tried not to feel disappointed with the inconclusive decision, reminding herself that accomplishing change took time and patience. Especially willing acceptance of change.

They had come a long way already with persistent patience and perseverance, and she intended to continue in the same manner. If they approached each other with open hearts and minds, they could find common ground.

She wouldn't stop until the local Amish community—a community bound by faith—reached the end of this journey.

❖ ❖ ❖

Lydia's heart sank, and her hands trembled, causing the letter she held to rustle and crinkle. Her mother had written with shocking and upsetting news from her family back in her former community: her youngest brother, Caleb, was suffering a serious illness. He was only fifteen, the blank page of his life yet unwritten. Lydia couldn't bear the thought of anything happening to him.

She had missed her mother and brothers since moving back to Lancaster County, and she felt suddenly pressed to visit them and see if there was anything she could do to help Caleb.

But what about the work I've been doing here to help find a compromise between the opposing factions and bring the conflict to an end? How can I abandon everyone here?

She realized the difficult decision she faced.

For months, she had poured her heart and soul into creating a bridge across the divide, working alongside Samuel, David, Ruth, and so many others to find common ground and build a future that respected both tradition and progress. The thought of leaving all her efforts behind pulled heavily on her heart, like a lead weight tied to a helium balloon. Her conflicting emotions and sense of duty in both cases waged war within her, and she felt cornered with indecision. She knew that she needed God's wisdom, guidance, and direction in this critical decision, and she poured out her heart to Him, acknowledging her inability to make a move without His help.

The next morning, she was glad to see Samuel

walk into the bakery. Perhaps God would use her talking with him to help her find peace about the right path.

"*Gude mariye*, Lydia," he greeted her with a smile. Then, seeming to sense her turmoil, his expression fell. "What's wrong?"

Aunt Martha bustled up beside her before she could form a reply. "Go and take a break, Lydia," she insisted.

Lydia had told her aunt and uncle about the contents of the letter she received from her mother, so the older woman knew the source of the worry that was distracting Lydia as she worked in the bakery.

When she edged around the counter, Samuel tenderly took her hand and led her to "their" table in the corner.

"Has something happened?" Samuel asked, keeping hold of her hand as they settled into the wooden ladder-back chairs.

"I've received news that my *bruder*, Caleb, is ill," Lydia answered, the hitch in her voice betraying her emotions. "I feel like my *familye* needs me there right now." She realized how she had said "there" and not "at home," which cemented in her heart what she already knew:

that her birth town and community had once again become her home. "How can I leave here, where these people also need me? I feel a sense of responsibility toward the *gmay* and toward the progress we've been making *and* to my *familye*, with Caleb so ill. I'm torn in two different directions and don't know what to do."

Samuel's face softened, his eyes filled with empathy. "I can't imagine how difficult this must be for you."

❋ ❋ ❋

Samuel couldn't believe that he was actually encouraging Lydia to go. But he put himself in her shoes and knew that were it him in the same situation, his responsibility to blood family would take precedence. And he knew it would be utterly selfish to advise her to turn her back on her family just because he wanted her to stay in Lancaster with him. Sometimes, a person's life took unexpected turns, and it was important to prioritize what truly mattered. Without a husband and father to lean on, Lydia's presence would bring comfort and strength to her mother and brothers during this difficult time.

Samuel pushed aside the nagging worry that if she left to return to her family, she might decide not to return to Lancaster County. He couldn't think about that.

Lydia nodded, unaware of his unspoken thoughts. "You're right, Samuel. I must go to them."

"When will you leave?" he asked.

"As soon as travel arrangements can be made. Caleb's illness is serious." Her usually bright blue eyes dulled with concern.

Samuel nodded abruptly. "Then you shouldn't waste any more time with me."

"Time with you is never wasted," she protested.

But she didn't resist when he stood to pull her to her feet and give her a brief hug before departing.

❈ ❈ ❈

Lydia told her aunt and uncle of her decision to return to her mother and brothers to support, serve, and love them during the challenging time they faced. Aunt Martha and Uncle Henry confirmed it was the right decision.

As Lydia packed her belongings a short time later, the upsetting thought of leaving the community she had grown to care about lingered in her mind. She couldn't help wondering when she might return.

Upon arriving at her mother's home, Lydia embraced the older woman, then exchanged hugs with her brothers. Caleb's illness was evident in his pale, sallow face and severe weight loss.

"I'm okay," he assured her when he noticed her eyeing him with concern. "A few days ago, I couldn't get out of bed, but I'm finally starting to feel a bit better. You didn't have to come."

"I wanted to come," she replied, relieved to hear he was improving. "And now that I'm here, I can make sure you continue on the road to recovery."

Later that night, Lydia sat in her old bedroom, her hands folded together in prayer. She asked for strength and healing to be bestowed upon Caleb. With the silent plea given, she felt a sense of peace wash over her, knowing that she would do all she could for her brother and that the rest was in the Lord's hands.

Over the course of the next week, Caleb's health continued to improve. He still hadn't gained all the weight back he lost during his illness and was weaker than he was when Lydia last saw him the previous fall, but she no longer feared the dreadful thought of his passing.

With concern for her brother no longer consuming her mind, her thoughts turned to Samuel. Oh, how she missed him! She yearned to return to him and resume the work she had left unfinished. Her aunt and uncle were likely missing her help at the bakery, too.

Lydia knew it was time to begin thinking about returning to Lancaster County.

She decided, though, that she would stay to visit with her family for a short while longer first before returning to Lancaster and determined not to allow so much time to pass before coming back to see them again. Though it was a lengthy journey, half a year was much too long to go without visiting her mother and brothers.

❋ ❋ ❋

With Lydia gone, Samuel's previously disregarded fears returned, wreaking havoc in his mind.

What if she doesn't come back?

He didn't believe that she would blithely abandon her self-apportioned mission, but her family needed her. And that took precedence over returning to Lancaster County to advocate for finding a compromise between the opposing factions.

Lydia started the ball rolling, but many others had joined her cause. They could carry on without her if necessary.

Yet, that didn't mean that Samuel wanted to do it without her by his side. She was the heart of the movement, and their spirit and drive seemed diminished without her. Or maybe it was only he who felt that way.

Lydia will come back eventually. I have to believe that. She moved to town to help her aunt and uncle, and she wouldn't turn her back on them. Even if she might not come back for my sake, she'll return to keep her promise to Martha and Henry Lapp.

Still, Samuel couldn't help wishing that she felt even a small measure of the same strong pull toward him that he felt toward her.

While Lydia was away from town visiting her family, Samuel spent most of his time at his family's farm, and he and Levi completed the spring planting. But keeping busy hadn't stopped him from missing her.

On Friday morning, Samuel pushed open the door to the Lapps' bakery, the familiar and comforting scent of freshly baked bread wafting out to greet him.

It was nearly two weeks since Lydia left to be with her family, and he had missed having her as a regular part of his day-to-day life. He certainly hadn't felt her absence to that degree when she left the first time all those years before. But back then, they only shared a childhood friendship. Now, however, she had come to mean so much more to him.

Samuel stepped inside the bakery, his gaze scanning the shop. He stopped short in surprise at the unexpected sight of Lydia standing behind the counter and filling the display case with pastries. He rushed forward to reach her. When she glanced up and spotted him, she set aside the tray and rounded the counter to meet him.

Samuel pulled her into a tight hug. "I'm so glad you're back," he said softly into her ear.

"I'm glad to be back," she replied.

He drew away slightly to look at her. "How is your *bruder*, Caleb?"

"He's doing much better. He's still a bit thin,

but my *maem* is determined to fatten him up with her *appeditlich* cooking."

"I'm happy to hear that Caleb is doing well again. That's *wunderbaar* news."

A throat cleared behind Lydia.

Samuel shifted his gaze to see Lydia's uncle standing behind her, the abandoned tray of pastries in his hand.

"If you would be so kind as to step aside, I can help our waiting customers," Henry said with a knowing smile that absolved any sting in his admonishment.

With a nod, Samuel led Lydia to their table.

Once seated, Samuel spent a few minutes catching Lydia up on all that had transpired while she was away. The truth was that not much changed, really. No progress had been made in bridging the two sides.

The committee had been more successful in winning concessions from the developer of the factory, who wanted to work with them to ensure that the *Englisch* company didn't alienate the local Amish community living in the area.

"David thinks we'll have a final proposal for everyone to vote on at the next community meeting," Samuel concluded.

A smile stretched across Lydia's face. "That's *gut* news. Now, we just have to convince enough people of the advantages of voting in favor of the factory."

Samuel reached across the table to take Lydia's hand, his heart swelling with affection for her. "You can count on me, Lydia. I'm always here for you, whatever you need."

"*Danki*, Samuel. I feel the same way about you." Before he could read more into those words than she had likely intended, she continued, "Having your support means so much to me. With you on my side, anything seems possible."

If anything is possible, does that mean there's a chance for more to grow between us than just friendship and a mutual partnership working together toward a common goal?

Samuel couldn't help but feel a glimmer of hope and anticipation for the possible future they might share.

CHAPTER ELEVEN

Lydia quickly fell back into the familiar routine at the bakery after returning to Lancaster and delighted in renewing the connections she had forged with Samuel and so many others in town. During her absence, she came to appreciate the strength of these bonds. Together, she and Samuel persevered in their efforts to bridge the divide between tradition and progress.

The road ahead wouldn't be without its difficulties, but with their shared commitment and support and given how much ground they had gained, Lydia was optimistic that they would succeed. She was not ignorant of the amount of plowing of hearts and sowing, watering, and nurturing of seeds that was still required, but she was a firm believer in being faithful and diligent in one's work to reap what they had sowed.

In addition to their efforts to reach a compromise about the proposed factory, plans for the community center were also progressing. The project, which had been put on hold for a number of weeks when everyone was focused on the relief efforts for the victims of the tornado, was back on track.

The community unanimously decided to build the center rather than trying to find an existing structure to use, and David Lantz had started working on drawing up a blueprint design in between meetings with the factory developer. A vacant plot of land near the main street of town had been donated by a local *Englisch* family who attended the auction the previous winter and had been inspired by the shared vision for the two communities. It was the ideal location, with a park directly across the street.

As Lydia and Samuel continued to collaborate on both projects, their relationship deepened. Samuel's unwavering presence had become a source of comfort and strength for her, and she found herself relying on his steady guidance and support more and more. They spent countless hours brainstorming ideas for the community center, envisioning the space that would serve as a hub for the Amish and *Englisch* communities to come together in harmony.

With each passing day, Lydia's admiration and fondness for Samuel grew. His kindness, wisdom, and genuine care for others resonated deeply with her. One evening, as the sun dipped toward the horizon, casting a brilliant wash of orange and pink across the sky and a golden glow over town, Lydia and Samuel walked from the bakery to the site where the community center was to be built.

They stood side by side, surveying the land that would soon be transformed into a gathering place for all the people in the area—a place where everyone was welcome, both Amish and *Englisch*.

"It's going to be *wunderbaar*," Lydia declared. "To think that this spot will soon be a physical symbol of unity and hope for our *gmay*."

Samuel nodded, a soft smile playing at the corners of his lips. "*Ya*, Lydia. It's a testament to the effectiveness of prayer, the power of collaboration, and the strength of our shared vision. I'm honored to be a part of it with you."

Lydia's heart skipped a beat at Samuel's words. A surge of emotion welled up within her, a connection to Samuel that went beyond the cords of friendship. She turned to look at Samuel. His gaze shifted to meet hers, and unspoken words hung in the air between them. But as the sun disappeared behind the hills to the west, Samuel glanced away from her, and the moment was lost.

That's if a moment was ever really there at all, thought Lydia. *Perhaps it was just my imagination thinking that there might be something more between us.*

She realized how much she had grown to care for Samuel and was subconsciously hoping he might reciprocate her affections.

"It's getting dark," he said, breaking into her musing. "We should head to your *aenti* and *onkel's* house so you're home before the last of the light fades."

Lydia made a noncommittal sound in response but allowed Samuel to escort her the short distance to Aunt Martha and Uncle Henry's house.

When they reached the front porch, she turned to say goodbye to him. "*Danki* for walking me here."

"*Gaern gschehne,*" he replied.

"I'll see you at the bakery on Friday," she added for no other reason than to extend her time with Samuel for even a few more moments.

"*Ya.* We can talk more about plans for the community center then."

She nodded in agreement.

They were both silent for the next several seconds.

"*Gude nacht*, Samuel," she said at last when she couldn't think of anything else to say to delay his departure any longer.

He echoed her words and watched as she headed inside.

Once she'd closed the door, Lydia immediately went to the front window, pulling aside the curtain in time to see him heading back toward the bakery, where he had left his horse and buggy. When he rounded the corner and disappeared from sight, she dropped the edge of the curtain again, sinking into a nearby chair and wondering if she'd merely imagined that moment she thought she and Samuel shared as the sun set and twilight fell.

❉ ❉ ❉

Later that night, Samuel sat in his living room gazing out the window over the dark landscape. Levi had gone to bed a short time earlier, but

Samuel remained up knowing he wouldn't be able to sleep.

His thoughts circled back once again for the umpteenth time to the moment he'd shared with Lydia at the site where the community center would be built. He wasn't sure why he had looked away. Was it because he worried he might be reading things into her actions that weren't really there? Had hope convinced him there was something profound between them when all she actually felt for him was friendship? Or was it possible that she felt as strongly for him as he did for her?

Turning away from the window, where he couldn't see anything anyway and wouldn't find any answers, his gaze fell on the worn Bible resting on the wooden table beside his chair. The gold lettering on the cover glinted in the lantern's glow.

Samuel reached to pick up the book and opened it, seeking solace in the words that had guided Believers and members of the Amish faith for generations. The pages fell open at a passage that seemed to speak directly to him.

"To every thing there is a season, and a time to every purpose under the heaven."

Samuel took a deep breath and settled back in

the chair, allowing the wisdom of those words to wash over him.

If he and Lydia were meant to be together, to build a life with each other as a family, it would happen in God's time, not his own. The Scripture verse reminded him of the need for patience and to yield himself and the desires of his heart to Him to guide Samuel's path.

Not only did the message speak directly to his relationship with Lydia, but it could also be applied to the situation surrounding the proposed factory.

The time to make a decision was drawing near. This was a pivotal moment in their history that would shape the future of their community. The tension caused by the *Englisch* company's plans for the land just outside of town still threatened to further fracture their unity.

A single question remained in Samuel's mind.

Will we be able to reach a compromise that will satisfy everybody? One that honors the traditions and values of the Amish while embracing growth and progress for the entire town?

Thoughts, a mix of hope and uncertainty, swirled through his mind. Nothing would be resolved that night, though. And he needed to get some rest since he'd have to be up early in the morning to tend to the animals.

In the following days, Samuel, Lydia, and other community members worked tirelessly to find a compromise that they hoped would receive the approval of both sides of the debate. They engaged in thoughtful discussions and careful negotiations. It was an onerous process navigating the complexities of different perspectives and deeply ingrained beliefs.

Samuel observed Lydia's unwavering determination and admired her resilience. She had a way of bringing people together, of finding common ground amidst opposing viewpoints. Her ability to listen and empathize with others made her a natural mediator, and it wasn't long before her efforts began to yield results once more.

* * *

When the final proposal was presented at the next community meeting, Lydia juggled a mixture of anticipation and apprehension.

What will they decide?

It felt as though the fate of their community hung in the balance.

This was her chance to bridge the divide between the opposing factions and offer a solution that would satisfy both the need for progress and the preservation of Amish traditions. The proposed factory challenged deeply ingrained beliefs, but it also held the promise of a brighter future for everyone.

She stood to address the room. "We stand at a crossroads today. For the past six months, I've heard the concerns and fears voiced by those who worry about the impact of the factory on our way of life. And I've also listened to the views of those who see it as an opportunity for growth and prosperity. We must consider the struggles our *gmay* faces and the opportunities that lie before us. I believe that we've found a way to honor our traditions while embracing progress." She spoke with passion and conviction, hoping that her words resonated with those gathered. "We propose a compromise that allows for the establishment of the factory while at the same time preserving *Amisch* customs. We've worked closely with the developer to ensure that their factory adheres to our values and respects our way of life. There will be regulations in place to protect our land, our traditions, and the environment.

These conditions will be a safeguard to ensure that the factory doesn't negatively impact our way of life. Together, we can forge a path that brings growth without sacrificing the identity of our *Amisch gmay*."

Lydia continued to outline the concessions the *Englisch* company was willing to make. The factory would be designed with architectural elements that blended seamlessly with the surrounding countryside, maintaining the aesthetic beauty of the area. The factory's operations would be conducted in a way that minimized noise and pollution, ensuring the tranquility of the community remained undisturbed. Additionally, a portion of the factory's profits would be allocated to support local businesses and initiatives, fostering economic stability within the community.

After Lydia finished speaking, she could see the impact of her words reflected on many of the faces around her. But had it been enough to sway the majority?

One by one, conservative and progressive members expressed their opinions about the developer's proposal. Some still held reservations, their concerns deeply rooted in their love for tradition and opposition to change. Others voiced their support, recognizing the need for progress and the potential benefits it could bring.

As the votes were tallied, the room fell into a hushed silence. When the results of the vote were announced, the proposal for the factory was accepted.

A mix of reactions revealed the people's responses, some bright with hope, and others merely resigned. A few displayed visible anger.

But the decision was made. The majority had chosen to move forward—toward a future that embraced change while maintaining their heritage. It was a moment of both triumph and reflection for Lydia.

Friends and neighbors had come together to make a difficult decision. The path ahead wouldn't be without challenges, but Lydia had faith in the community's ability to adapt and preserve what was truly important.

Samuel's mouth turned up in a smile. "You did it, Lydia. You helped us find a way through a deadlock. A way that honors both the past and the future. I admire your strength and unwavering commitment to our community."

The smile that graced her own face was

as much from relief as happiness. Though she had not allowed herself to dwell on thoughts of failing, she could acknowledge in retrospect that the possibility of her efforts not being met with success was very real.

Her aunt had told her of others who tried to implement changes but were thwarted, and Lydia was glad to have helped bring about a different outcome this time. "I couldn't have done it without your support, Samuel. And the support of so many others. Together, we've shown that when we listen to one another and work toward a common goal, we can overcome even the most daunting of obstacles."

CHAPTER TWELVE

Samuel stood surrounded by the rolling landscape, watching as the construction crews began their work on the factory site. The once-empty field was now a bustling hive of activity with machinery and workers in hard hats going about their various jobs. The sound of the gas engines and equipment as they broke ground echoed across the countryside. The project was underway, and many had come out to watch the progress.

Members of the Amish community observed the construction process with a sense of wonder and cautious anticipation. Some members still held reservations, their fear of change lingering. But others, like Samuel, had come to view the project as a symbol of unity and willingness to adapt.

Standing beside Lydia and David, Samuel felt

a mix of emotions as he witnessed the physical manifestation of the community's decision. They had worked for many months to ensure that the construction plans respected the values and traditions of the Amish community, and now their effects were being realized.

He couldn't help but feel a sense of pride for Lydia and the others who championed the cause. They had proven that not all progress and tradition were mutually exclusive but could sometimes successfully coexist in harmony. He looked around, his heart swelling with love for his community and admiration for Lydia, David, and all those who had worked selflessly to make this vision a reality.

Soon, the foundations would be laid, and after that, the framework would start to take shape. Through it all, Samuel, Lydia, and David would remain on hand to guide the project.

In the coming months, there would be meetings with the construction teams, architects, and project managers, ensuring that all the agreements made with the developer were followed. As he thought about all the work ahead and the pivotal role Lydia would continue to play in it, Samuel's admiration for her grew even more. She had shown him a new way of looking at the world, one that embraced change without sacrificing their beliefs. Her determination and unwavering commitment to their community inspired him. He found himself falling more and more in love with her each day.

But could he find the courage to confess his feelings for her?

And was there any hope that she might love him in return?

❉ ❉ ❉

Lydia stood at the edge of the construction site, a smile playing on her lips as she watched the official groundbreaking for the factory. It was a tangible representation of the community's ability to embrace change while remaining true to their traditions.

She felt Samuel's presence beside her, and she reached out to take his hand, turning her head to look at him.

"It's incredible, isn't it?" he said, interlacing his fingers with hers. His gaze remained fixed on the workers rather than meeting hers as he continued. "What can be achieved by working together is truly amazing. I never thought I would see the day when our *gmay* would embark on such a venture. But seeing the positive impact it's having, I can't help but be thankful for it."

Lydia nodded in agreement even though he couldn't see her action with his eyes still focused on the scene in front of them. "Change can be daunting, but it can also open doors we never knew existed."

Samuel finally turned toward her, a softness in his eyes that she had never noticed before. "*Danki* for taking me on this journey with you."

"I couldn't have been happier to have anyone else by my side." She paused.

Did that even make sense? "I couldn't have been happier if I'd had anyone else by my side." Is that any better? What I meant is that there is no one I'd rather have had by my side than Samuel.

Fortunately, he seemed to grasp her meaning because his face lit up with a smile. Lydia's heart swelled with an overabundance of feelings. Friendship. Care. And something deeper. She had always admired Samuel's strong connection to his Amish roots, but seeing him embrace the positive impact of the factory filled her with even more warm emotions.

At the end of the week, the community members gathered to celebrate the groundbreaking of the factory. Lydia sat beside Samuel, their friends and neighbors around them. The room was filled with a sense of camaraderie and accomplishment as Mr. Troyer stood up to speak, praising the collaborations that had made the factory possible.

"Today, we celebrate not just the start of construction but the triumph of unity over division. When it is completed, the factory will stand as a testament to the resilience of our *gmay*, our commitment to our values, our faith in *Gott*, and our willingness to adapt without compromising who we are. Now, the developer has an announcement to make. So, I'll give the floor to Ms. Armstrong, the company CEO."

An older woman with short gray hair cut into a chin-length bob stepped forward. "It's been an honor to work with the local Amish community over the past few months. I've seen the dedication and pride in the work of the Amish craftsmen and women in town firsthand. That's why I'm pleased to announce that we will be partnering with local Amish-owned businesses to supply materials for the factory. This ensures that our company respects the values and traditions of the Amish while also supporting the local economy."

Gasps of surprise and excited murmurs spread through the gathering, expressions igniting with joy and relief. Lydia was just as elated as everyone else, knowing that this new partnership would not only provide business opportunities for many but also strengthen the bond between the Amish and *Englisch* communities.

She turned to Samuel. "Can you believe it? Our *gmay* is embracing change in ways we never thought possible."

Samuel reached out to clasp her hand, a broad smile on his face. "If I still had any doubts that this was the right path forward—which I don't"— he interrupted himself to reassure her— "then this announcement would have obliterated them."

They had bridged the divide in their community, overcoming resistance and embracing change. And together, they would continue to nurture the bonds that had grown between the Amish and *Englisch* residents in town.

I only hope that the bond between me and Samuel will be strengthened, too, Lydia mused to herself.

❋ ❋ ❋

Samuel looked around at all the people gathered. A sharp pang that his brother was not among the crowd pierced him. Samuel and Levi had come to a tentative truce after the decision about the factory was made by the community. The brothers' opposing views didn't matter any longer—insomuch as it wouldn't alter the outcome of whether or not the factory would be built. The town had issued the permits for the construction, and the developer was moving forward with their plans.

Not surprisingly, Levi had refused to come to the celebration of the groundbreaking. He and his group of conservative friends who voted against the factory also boycotted the event, claiming that the project was nothing to celebrate.

And Samuel had no doubt that if he and Lydia and the others didn't follow through on ensuring that the promises made to the Amish community were kept, Samuel and Levi would be at odds again and tensions between them would resume, with Levi voicing his opinions anew about the dangers of the *Englisch* world encroaching on their traditions.

But Samuel didn't want to consider such negative thoughts right then. It was an occasion that was meant to be joyful, and it was—despite the absence of a small fraction of their community.

Turning to look at Lydia, his spirits lifted, an irrepressible sense of awe at the woman who had captivated his heart filling him. Their renewed childhood friendship developed during their shared endeavors into something deeper and more profound. For him, at least. And he hoped for her, too.

Samuel's heart swelled with gratitude that the Lord had placed him on the path that led him to this moment. As he gazed at Lydia, he felt increasingly certain that their shared journey had shaped not only the community but their relationship as well.

It dawned on him that love wasn't just about finding someone who shared his beliefs—it was about finding someone who challenged, inspired, and supported him, allowing him to become the best version of himself.

CHAPTER THIRTEEN

Hannah Fisher sat alone in her room at her parents' farmhouse, her mind awhirl with conflicting thoughts and emotions. She was home from college for the summer—but that was all. She hadn't told anyone yet—not even her younger sister, Ruth—that she was going to pursue a career in nursing.

Truth be told, she was anxious about her family's reaction when she finally did announce her plans. Yet, she knew that would only be a small hurdle compared to the reactions of the more conservative members of the local Amish community. Many of them didn't support her decision to go to college in the first place, believing that she would be influenced by the outside world. And maybe they'd been right to be concerned about that.

The life that once felt so familiar and reassuring to Hannah now felt constricting. She questioned if she would ever find contentment in the kind of traditional Amish life that was expected of her by her family and community. The truth was, Hannah had always felt a yearning for something beyond the boundaries of their community. She had dreams and ambitions that stretched beyond the simplicity of their lifestyle.

Her time away from the Amish community had afforded her experiences and opportunities that gave her a sense of purpose. She'd missed her family and friends while she was gone, living so far away from them. But she felt a sense of freedom and independence, too.

Hannah had started working at a hospital as part of the practical coursework for one of her classes, and she found that she derived deep satisfaction from helping people in this setting and making a difference in their lives. The idea of caring for others and having a purpose beyond the limitations of her community greatly appealed to her.

When she returned to school in the fall, she intended to enroll in a nursing course. And sometime between then and now, she would have to tell her family. But she wasn't yet ready to do so.

Hannah rose and sauntered over to the window, pulling back the curtain to look at the rolling pastures and fields of her family's farm. From her vantage point on the second floor, she could see the farmhouse where Samuel lived with his brother since their land bordered her parents' property.

Hannah had seen Samuel with Lydia a few times in town. She couldn't help but notice the growing closeness between the two. Their smiles and laughter were undeniable proof of the connection they had forged—more than just the friendship Hannah remembered them sharing as children at school.

She was truly happy that Samuel had found someone so wonderful and wondered if he and Lydia were starting to make a life together and planning a shared future already.

Hannah and Samuel's futures had diverged a long time ago. They were on different paths, and she didn't foresee them ever reconnecting again, not in any significant way. But she hoped they could remain friends.

They both deserved to pursue the lives that

would bring them fulfillment, albeit in different directions. She hoped to find her own place of contentment where her passion for helping others could thrive.

She knew that her choice would lead her away from the life she was born into, but she couldn't help feeling anticipation for the possibilities that lay ahead.

She released the curtain to drift back into place over the window and decided to go for a walk. She made it out of the house without encountering her mother or Ruth or her youngest sister, Mary.

Hannah set off at a brisk pace, giving a wide berth to the large barn behind the farmhouse so she wouldn't risk running into her father or younger brother, Noah. She meandered slowly across the pasture with no particular destination in mind. She wasn't really paying attention to the scenery in any case, as the focus of her thoughts was turned inward.

The Amish way of life had provided her with a strong sense of community and belonging, but lately, she couldn't shake the feeling that she no longer fit in. The traditional expectations felt stifling and limiting rather than comforting. The thought of learning and growing, of embracing a world where she could truly be of help to others, filled her with a renewed sense of purpose.

But with these dreams also came the weight of uncertainty. Pursuing a career in the outside world meant leaving behind everything she had ever known while growing up—and risked separating her from her family and community.

Hannah's wandering didn't help to settle her thoughts any, and she finally decided to turn around and begin making her way back home.

Nee, *back to my* eldre's *farmhouse,* she corrected herself.

The room she rented near the community college during the school year didn't feel like a home, but she couldn't keep referring to Lancaster County as home either since she had decided to establish a life away from there.

Hannah contemplated her future, aware that she couldn't ignore the longing in her heart and calling to continue on the current course she had set for herself.

❊ ❊ ❊

Samuel finished replacing some rotted boards in the wooden fence marking the border between his land and the Fishers' farm. Glancing up, he noticed Hannah walking nearby on the other side of the fence.

He called out in greeting, and she changed direction to head toward him.

"*Gude daag*, Samuel," she greeted.

He leaned on the fence separating them, crossing his arms on the top rail. "I guess you'll be going back to school soon."

"*Ya*. I'm only here for a short visit with my *familye*." She reached up to tuck a loose strand of curly blond hair behind her ear. "I saw you and Lydia together in town at Ruth's gallery the other day."

"*Ach*?" he replied, not wanting to make things awkward and so allowing her to take the lead on commenting on seeing him with Lydia for a second time.

"I didn't greet you since you didn't notice me," she replied ruefully, softening her words with a smile. "You were completely focused on Lydia. You two seem close."

He straightened away from the fence and gripped the top rail with his hands. "Does that bother you?"

Hannah shook her head in rebuttal. "*Nee*. You

and I are better off as friends. And as your friend, I want you to find happiness, whether that's with Lydia or someone else. Not that you need my approval, of course. But I think Lydia is good for you." She offered him another soft smile. "*Mach's gut*, Samuel."

As she walked away, he resumed his work, but his mind immediately turned to thoughts of Lydia. She was so different from Hannah. Not just in appearance but also with respect to Hannah's desire to make a life away from their Amish community rather than within it, such as Lydia was doing.

Samuel's feelings for Lydia had grown deeper with the passing of time, and there was no denying that he loved her. The question now was what to do about it.

Because Lydia had returned to the community from the visit to her family, he no longer feared it would be a repeat of the situation with Hannah, following the same pattern with her heart constantly being pulled elsewhere and her leaving for extended periods with Samuel always waiting for her.

But if that's the case and my doubts and reservations are no longer applicable, then what's holding me back from revealing my feelings to Lydia?

It was still fear that was keeping him from forging ahead—though not for the same reason as before.

Now, his fear was that Lydia might not feel the same way about him. He thought he had seen signs of requited deeper feelings from her, but what if he confessed his love for her, only to be told that she viewed him as just a friend? How could he continue to work with her and spend time in her company after opening himself up to her in that way and not have his feelings reciprocated?

But if I don't take the risk, I might miss the chance of building a life with her. I want to marry her and one day start a familye *with her.*

The first step toward securing that future would be declaring his intentions and courting her. And even if these past few months had felt very much like a courtship, that didn't make it official.

Assuming she agrees.

He was back to doubting. Samuel decided then and there that the next time he saw her, he wouldn't allow them to part again without first professing his feelings for her.

And if he broke out in a cold sweat at the

thought, he'd cross that bridge when he got to it and not dwell on it beforehand, just as he ignored his suddenly pounding heart. Both of those could be attributed to him doing physical labor outside on a warm June day.

Taking a deep breath, he closed his eyes and prayed for courage and calmness. He would trust that *Gott* was guiding his path. And it seemed that each step was leading him straight to Lydia.

If he was fortunate enough to have her love, it would be a blessing that he vowed he would cherish every day for the rest of his life.

❊ ❊ ❊

Samuel came into the bakery, and Lydia greeted him with a smile. "*Gude daag*, Samuel."

"*Gude daag*, Lydia," he returned.

His arrival wasn't a surprise, as she was expecting him. The two of them would be meeting David and Ruth that afternoon to discuss plans for the community center, and Lydia and Samuel had agreed to walk there together from the bakery.

"Are you ready to go?" asked Samuel.

"Just a minute." She finished wiping crumbs from the counter and deposited them in a trash can before disappearing into the back room to wash her hands and collect the basket of food she'd packed earlier.

She and Samuel had decided to share a picnic lunch in the park across the street from the vacant plot of land after they finished the meeting with David and Ruth. Lydia intended to invite the couple to join them, so she'd included extra sandwiches made from freshly baked bread.

Calling out a goodbye to her aunt, Lydia let the older woman know that she was leaving.

"Take your time," Aunt Martha said. "There's no need to rush back. Your *onkel* should be here in a few minutes to help me with the lunch rush. It used to be just the two of us doing all the work at the bakery, and even though we're getting older, we can still make do on our own for a few hours."

"*Danki, Aenti.*"

Samuel held the door open for Lydia, and she stepped outside ahead of him. They set off together toward the site of the future town community center.

It was just before noon, and the sun shone brightly overhead. A light breeze kept the June day from being too warm. Flowerboxes lined the storefronts along the street, overflowing with a profusion of vivid purples and pinks amidst the greenery.

Lydia and Samuel exchanged greetings with people they passed on the sidewalk but didn't linger so that they wouldn't be late for the meeting and keep David and Ruth waiting.

To the west, the havoc that the tornado had wreaked was still visible on the landscape, but the farmhouses scattered across the countryside stood tall and complete once again where they'd been for generations, thanks to the community's rebuilding efforts.

When Lydia and Samuel reached the community center site, they found David and Ruth already there. Lydia set down the basket on the ground off to one side so it would be out of the way.

As they all exchanged greetings, she noticed that David had a long roll of papers tucked under his arm. Once the pleasantries were over, David unfurled the large sheets of paper. Samuel took hold of one side, while David held the other to keep the edges of the pages from curling closed.

Lydia inched closer to Samuel to get a better look at the blueprints of the initial design David had come up with. She didn't understand what all of the symbols meant initially until David kindly explained them to her. She started to envision how the flat two-dimensional building on the page would look once complete, coming to life in front of them where only a vacant lot currently stood.

As they discussed various aspects, suggestions were proposed, and several changes were made. The more they talked, the clearer the community center took shape in Lydia's mind.

"I think we should have one exterior wall without any windows," Ruth recommended.

"Why?" Samuel asked, his brow furrowing at the odd request. "We want the space to be light and bright, don't we?"

Ruth immediately elaborated. "We can make the windows bigger throughout the rest of the building to compensate. But I'd like a large solid expanse because it will allow me to create a mural on one of the outside walls of the community center, showing a scene of Amish and *Englisch* working together."

"What a *wunderbaar* idea," Lydia praised.

"I agree," David seconded.

"*Ya*, me, too," Samuel added, making it unanimous.

David rolled up the blueprints and secured them with a rubber band. "I'll make the alterations, and we can meet again in a week to review them again before showing the design to the other committee members."

His words were met with nods of agreement.

As David and Ruth prepared to take their leave, Lydia asked if the couple would like to join her and Samuel for a picnic lunch.

"*Danki*, but *nee*," Ruth replied. "I need to head back to the gallery. I usually have several patrons visiting during lunch hour."

David declined as well. "I'd like to get to work on the design changes we discussed."

They both bade all farewell, leaving Lydia and Samuel alone.

"Are you ready to eat," he asked.

"*Ya*."

He retrieved the basket of food and reached for her hand as they crossed the street to the park. Lydia kept her fingers entwined with his, allowing him to lead her across the grassy expanse to the gazebo at the center. They sat down on the built-in wooden bench that ran parallel to the gazebo wall inside. She was finally forced to release his hand when she needed to take the food out of the basket.

As they ate, they talked more about the plans for the community center. Lydia mentioned planning another charity event to raise funds to cover the building costs that exceeded whatever donations they received.

"I was thinking we could have a craft fair at the weekend farmer's market. Lots of people come to support it from all the surrounding areas, and I can organize a group of women—and even men—to make the crafts. We could sell handmade items such as quilts, knitted items, rag dolls, and wooden carvings. What do you think of that idea?"

He nodded in agreement, but she noticed he seemed distracted and wondered what was on his mind. She didn't press him on it, however, figuring that if it was something he wanted to share with her, he'd do so when he was ready.

Once they were finished with lunch, Lydia packed the uneaten food back into the basket.

"I should be getting back to the bakery." She started to stand up, but Samuel halted her movement with a hand on her arm.

"Lydia, wait. There's something that I'd like to say to you."

She sank back down onto the bench. "What is it?"

Apprehension flittered through her at his word choice. Something to *tell* her rather than talk to her about. Which meant it likely didn't concern one of the projects they were working on together.

What else could he want to say?

CHAPTER FOURTEEN

The sky overhead, unmarred by a single cloud, was the same brilliant shade of blue as Lydia's eyes. Samuel felt overly warm sitting in the gazebo at the park, but it had little to do with the mild heat of the day. Instead, it was because of the woman beside him—or more specifically, thoughts about her reaction to the words he intended to say to her. That is, if he could find the courage to voice them.

He had spent countless hours working alongside Lydia for many months. The bond they forged in their joint efforts was strong, and he couldn't let this moment slip away without expressing his true feelings.

Samuel took a deep breath, his heart pounding in his chest as he searched for the right words.

"Lydia, I've cherished our friendship since we were *kinner*. And now, spending time with you again, I've come to feel so much more for you. Your strength, compassion, and unwavering faith have touched my heart in ways I never thought possible. I've fallen in love with you."

Surprise and astonishment flashed across her face. "You love me?"

"I do." So much that words were not enough to describe it. But he wanted to try. "I'm blessed to have you in my life."

"I feel the same way about you."

"Which part of it."

"All of it," she said with a tender smile. "I love you too, Samuel."

The breath he didn't even realize he'd been holding gusted forth from his chest. "I want to build a life with you. I'd like to start courting with that intention. To explore the depths of our connection and see where our journey leads us."

Lydia's blue eyes shimmered with emotion as she met his gaze. Her lips curved up further into a broad smile, but then her joy suddenly dimmed. "How will Levi react to a courtship between us?"

Not well, likely.

Though Samuel didn't voice the thought

aloud, Lydia had obviously come to the same conclusion.

"Perhaps we should keep it a secret for the time being," she suggested.

"We'd have to keep it a secret from everyone, then. Otherwise, word of it could get back to Levi."

Lydia wouldn't even be able to tell her aunt and uncle, but if that thought bothered her, it didn't show on her face. "I know."

"Does that mean you agree to begin courting?"

"*Ya.*"

He leaned forward and placed a soft kiss on her lips.

When he drew back, Lydia glanced around quickly. "I don't think anyone saw us."

He wished he could shout from the rooftops about his feelings for Lydia. But for the time being, it was enough that she knew.

A wave of relief washed over him that he had been able to speak his heart to her and that he was not met by disappointment regarding her feelings for him. A smile spread across his face, thinking about how she loved him, too, and he couldn't contain his joy.

With a quick glance around to ensure that they were still alone in the park, Samuel gently cupped Lydia's face in his hands and leaned forward to kiss her again, his lips brushing against hers. It was a kiss filled with tenderness and the promise of a future together.

Lydia returned the kiss without hesitation, but when it ended, she immediately placed her hands over his and pulled their interlocked fingers down to her lap. "You better stop doing that in the middle of town where someone could see us—unless you don't want our courtship to be a secret after all."

"I don't want to keep things secret," he admitted. "But right now, it's for the best to keep it just between us. I want Levi to get to know you a little more, and I don't want his possible disapproval to mar our happiness."

And he was happy despite the obstacles that remained.

"I wish we could share our joy with all our friends and *familye*," Lydia commented.

"So do I. It won't have to stay a secret forever," he assured her. "One day, Levi will realize how *wunderbaar* you are, just as I do, and then he'll love you as a *schweschder*."

Coming to an understanding about things, Samuel's heart felt lighter, as did Lydia's. Besides,

Lydia's heart was so buoyed up on a sea of joy that Samuel loved her in return that she couldn't give any thoughts about his brother more than a second's notice. Chirping birds and the sweet scent of blossoming flowers filled the air, creating the perfect backdrop for Samuel's declaration of love for her and the start of their courtship.

"I never expected to develop such a deep bond with you when I came back to town last fall," she said, continuing to hold his hands in hers.

His eyes crinkled at the corners as he grinned widely. "Neither did I. You are a ray of light in my life. From the moment we met after so many years apart, I felt a connection with you that I couldn't explain."

A warm surge of emotion washed over Lydia at his words. "It was the same for me," she admitted. "I never thought I would find someone who understands and supports me the way you do, Samuel." Lydia's eyes sparkled as she squeezed his hands. "The road we've traveled hasn't always been easy, but it has brought us so much closer. Together, we have proven that unity can be found in the most unexpected places."

Samuel sensed that Lydia was speaking not only about the community but the two of them as well, and his feelings matched Lydia's. In a short time, he had come to see her as a remarkable woman and as a true partner—someone together with whom he could face life's joys and challenges.

"Lydia, I never imagined that our journey would be filled with such wide-ranging trials and triumphs. But I'm grateful for every moment we've spent together and for the way you opened my eyes to the possibilities of change."

In that moment, Lydia felt an overwhelming sense of gratitude for the twists and turns that led her to that point. Deep in her heart, she knew that she had found her soulmate. They would embrace the future together and continue their mutual journey, united by faith in God, love, and their shared vision of the future of their community. The factory project and the community center were only the first of many things they would do together. They would navigate all of life's ups and downs, guided by love and trust in the Lord.

As they sat, hand in hand, Samuel marveled that their journey together was only just beginning. He prayed that he would be able to spend a lifetime with her. And as he looked into Lydia's eyes and saw the love he felt for her mirrored there, Samuel couldn't help but feel a renewed sense of hope. He had vowed to let go of his past, and through Lydia, he built a bridge of progress and discovered a future worth fighting for.

❊ ❊ ❊

Did you enjoy your trip to Lancaster County? Find out more of what happens to Hannah, Ruth, Samuel, and Lydia. The Lancaster Bridges series explores a close-knit Amish community in Pennsylvania as they navigate the challenges of a rapidly changing world. Experience the beauty and simplicity of Amish culture, while also witnessing the characters' journeys of self-discovery, personal growth, and community building. Overall, the series offers a rich and heartfelt portrayal of a community that is both deeply traditional and open to change, and celebrates the enduring values of family, faith, and love.

❊ ❊ ❊

The Bridge of Solace (Lancaster Bridges Book 3)
When a young Amish man, Daniel Byler, returns to the community after serving time in prison, he finds an unlikely ally in Lydia Lapp, who sees his potential for change and growth. As Lydia's efforts to bridge the gap between the Amish and *Englisch* communities continue, she organizes a community event that brings together members from both worlds.

Meanwhile, Hannah Fisher continues to grapple with her own struggles outside of the community and finds solace in her work at the hospital, where she meets a kind and caring *Englisch* doctor. As the relationships between the characters deepen, secrets are revealed, and the community faces opposition to their progress. Will they be able to overcome the challenges and continue to move forward while still respecting Amish values and traditions?

❊ ❊ ❊

The Bridge of Forgiveness (Lancaster Bridges Book 4)
The Bridge of Belonging (Lancaster Bridges Book 5)

Thank you, readers!

Thank you for reading this book. It is important to me to share my stories with you and that you enjoy them. May I ask a favor of you? If you enjoyed this book, would you please take a moment to leave a review on Amazon and/or Goodreads? Thank you for your support!

Also, each week, I send my readers updates about my life as well as information about my new releases, freebies, promos, and book recommendations. If you're interested in receiving my weekly newsletter, please go to newsletter.sylviaprice.com, and it will ask you for your email. As a thank-you, you will receive several FREE exclusive short stories that aren't available for purchase!

Blessings,
Sylvia

BOOKS BY THIS AUTHOR

Sarah (The Amish Of Morrissey County Prequel)

Available for FREE on Amazon

Welcome to Morrissey County! This fictional region in Pennsylvania Amish country is home to several generations of strong-willed Amish women who know what they want in life, even if others disagree. Join these women on their search for love and acceptance.

Morrissey County, 1979

Sarah Kauffman has always abided by the Ordnung, and not only because her father happens to be the town's bishop and would, she feels, disown her if she didn't. But when her mother passes away, she longs to escape the clutches of her father and run away to the Englisch world.

When her father wants her to marry someone she doesn't love, Sarah becomes even more desperate to leave.

Jacob Renno, on the other hand, is happy with life on his farm. It keeps him so busy that the older bachelor has no time for love, but on lonely nights, he finds himself longing for a companion.

When Sarah and Jacob meet, there's an instant connection, but things get complicated. Jacob offers to help Sarah with her dilemma, but Bishop Kaufmann insists that she obey his wishes. Will Sarah run off to join the Englisch, or will the handsome farmer give her pause? Will her father disown her or give her his blessing? Find out in this sweet Amish romance as you become immersed in the lives of these Morrissey County residents.

Sarah is the prequel to the Amish of Morrissey County series. Each book is a stand-alone read, but to make the most of the series, you should consider reading them in order.

The Origins Of Cardinal Hill (The Amish Of Cardinal Hill Prequel)

Available for FREE on Amazon

Two girls with a legacy to carry on. A third

choosing to forge her own path.

Welcome to Cardinal Hill, Indiana! This quaint fictional town is home to Faith Hochstetler, Leah Bontrager, Iris Mast, their families, and their trades. Faith, Leah, and Iris are united in their shared passion for turning their hobbies within nature into profitable businesses...and finding love! Find out how it all begins in this short, free prequel!

Other books in this series:
The Beekeeper's Calendar: Faith's Story
The Soapmaker's Recipe: Leah's Story
The Herbalist's Remedy: Iris's Story

The Origins of Cardinal Hill is the prequel to the Amish of Cardinal Hill series. Each book is a stand-alone read, but to make the most of the series, you should consider reading them in order.

A Promised Tomorrow (The Yoder Family Saga Prequel)

Available for FREE on Amazon

The Yoder Family Saga follows widow Miriam Yoder and her four unmarried daughters, Megan, Rebecca, Josephine, and Lillian, as they discover God's plans for them and the hope He provides for a happy tomorrow.

The Yoder women struggle to survive after Jeremiah Yoder succumbs to a battle with cancer. The family risks losing their farm and their livelihood. They are desperate to find a way to keep going. Will Miriam and her daughters be able to work together to keep their family afloat? Will God pull through for them and provide for them in their time of need?

A Promised Tomorrow is the prequel to the Yoder Family Saga. Join the Yoder women through their journey of loss and hope for a better future. Each book is a stand-alone read, but to make the most of the series, you should consider reading them in order. Start reading this sweet Amish romance today that will take you on a rollercoaster of emotions as you're welcomed into the life of the Yoder family.

The Christmas Cards: An Amish Holiday Romance

Lucy Yoder is a young Amish widow who recently lost the love of her life, Albrecht. As Christmas approaches, she dreads what was once her favorite holiday, knowing that this Christmas was supposed to be the first one she and Albrecht shared together. Then, one December morning, Lucy discovers a Christmas card from an anonymous sender on her doorstep. Lucy receives more cards, all personal, all tender, all comforting.

Who in the shadows is thinking of her at Christmas?

Andy Peachey was born with a rare genetic disorder. Coming to grips with his predicament makes him feel a profound connection to Lucy Yoder. Seeking meaning in life, he uses his talents to give Christmas cheer. Will Andy's efforts touch Lucy's heart and allow her to smile again? Or will Lucy, herself, get in his way?

The Christmas Cards is a story of loss and love and the ability to find yourself again in someone else. Instead of waiting for each part to be released, enjoy the entire Christmas Cards series in this exclusive collection!

The Christmas Arrival: An Amish Holiday Romance

Rachel Lapp is a young Amish woman who is the daughter of the community's bishop. She is in the midst of planning the annual Christmas Nativity play when newcomer Noah Miller arrives in town to spend Christmas with his cousins. Encouraged by her father to welcome the new arrival, Rachel asks Noah to be a part of the Nativity.

Despite Rachel's engagement to Samuel King, a local farmer, she finds herself irrevocably drawn to Noah and his carefree spirit. Reserved and slightly shy, Noah is hesitant to get involved in the play, but an unlikely friendship begins to develop between Rachel and Noah, bringing with it unexpected problems, including a seemingly harmless prank with life-threatening consequences that require a Christmas miracle.

Will Rachel honor her commitment to Samuel, or will Noah win her affections?

Join these characters on what is sure to be a heartwarming holiday adventure! Instead of waiting for each part to be released, enjoy the entire Christmas Arrival series at once!

Amish Love Through The Seasons (The Complete Series)

Featuring many of the beloved characters from Sylvia Price's bestseller, The Christmas Arrival, as well as a new cast of characters, Amish Love Through the Seasons centers around a group of teenagers as they find friendship, love, and hope in the midst of trials. ***This special boxed set includes the entire series, plus a bonus companion story, "Hope for Hannah's Love."***

Tragedy strikes a small Amish community outside of Erie, Pennsylvania when Isaiah Fisher, a widower and father of three, is involved in a serious accident. When his family is left scrambling to pick up the pieces, the community unites to help the single father, but the hospital bills keep piling up. How will the family manage?

Mary Lapp, a youth in the community, decides to take up Isaiah's cause. She enlists the help of other teenagers to plant a garden and sell the produce. While tending to the garden, new relationships develop, but old ones are torn apart. With tensions mounting, will the youth get past their disagreements in order to reconcile and produce fruit? Will they each find love? Join them on their adventure through the seasons!

Included in this set are all the popular titles:
Seeds of Spring Love
Sprouts of Summer Love
Fruits of Fall Love
Waiting for Winter Love
"Hope for Hannah's Love" (a bonus companion short story)

Jonah's Redemption (Book 1)

Available for FREE on Amazon

Jonah has lost his community, and he's struggling to get by in the English world. He yearns for his Amish roots, but his past mistakes keep him from returning home.

Mary Lou is recovering from a medical scare. Her journey has impressed upon her how precious life is, so she decides to go on rumspringa to see the world.

While in the city, Mary Lou meets Jonah. Unable to understand his foul attitude, especially towards her, she makes every effort to share her faith with him. As she helps him heal from his past, an attraction develops.

Will Jonah's heart soften towards Mary Lou? What will God do with these two broken people?

Elijah: An Amish Story Of Crime And Romance

He's Amish. She's not. Each is looking for a change. What happens when God brings them together?

Elijah Troyer is eighteen years old when he decides to go on a delayed Rumspringa, an Amish tradition when adolescents venture out into the world to decide whether they want to continue their life in the Amish culture or leave for the ways of the world. He has only been in the city for a month when his life suddenly takes a strange twist.

Eve Campbell is a young woman in trouble with crime lords, and they will do anything to stop her from talking. After a chance encounter, Elijah is drawn into Eve's world at the same time she is drawn into his heart. He is determined to help Eve escape from the grips of her past, but his Amish upbringing has not prepared him for the dangers he encounters as he tries to pull Eve from her chaotic world and into his peaceful one.

Will Elijah choose to return to the safety of his family, or will the ways of the world sink their hooks into him? Do Elijah and Eve have a chance at a future together? Find out in this action-packed standalone novel.

Finding Healing (Rainbow Haven Beach Prequel)

Available for FREE on Amazon

Discover the power of second chances in this heartwarming series about love, loss, and a fresh start from bestselling author Sylvia Price.

After the death of her husband, Beth Campbell decides it's time for a fresh start. When she returns to her hometown in Nova Scotia, she discovers a beautiful old abandoned home by the seaside and imagines it as the perfect spot for her to run a bed and breakfast and finally have the chance to write a novel. But when she discovers that the house belongs to Sean Pennington, a man with whom she has a painful history, she begins to doubt her dream.

With the encouragement of her friends and newfound faith, Beth takes a chance on the dilapidated home and hires Sean as a skilled carpenter to help her restore it. As they work together to bring the old house back to life, Beth and Sean's shared history resurfaces, forcing them to confront unresolved feelings and past mistakes. Will they be able to forgive each other and move on, or will their complicated history keep them apart?

Join Beth on her journey of self-discovery and forgiveness. This inspirational series will touch your heart and remind you that it's never too late to start again. It is perfect for fans of uplifting women's fiction and readers who enjoy stories of finding hope and joy in unexpected places.

Songbird Cottage Beginnings (Pleasant Bay Prequel)

Available for FREE on Amazon

Set on Canada's picturesque Cape Breton Island, this book is perfect for those who enjoy new beginnings and countryside landscapes.

Sam MacAuley and his wife Annalize are total opposites. When Sam wants to leave city life in

Halifax to get a plot of land on Cape Breton Island, where he grew up, his wife wants nothing to do with his plans and opts to move herself and their three boys back to her home country of South Africa.

As Sam settles into a new life on his own, his friend Lachlan encourages him to get back into the dating scene. Although he meets plenty of women, he longs to find the one with whom he wants to share the rest of his life. Will Sam ever meet "the one"?

Get to know Sam and discover the origins of the Songbird Cottage. This is the prequel to the rest of the Pleasant Bay series.

The Crystal Crescent Inn Boxed Set (Sambro Lighthouse Complete Series)

Amazon bestselling author Sylvia Price's Sambro Lighthouse Series, set on Canada's picturesque Crystal Crescent Beach, is a feel-good read perfect for fans of second chances with a bit of history and mystery all rolled into one. Enjoy all five sweet romance books in one collection for the first time!

Liz Beckett is grief-stricken when her beloved husband of thirty-five years dies after a long battle with cancer. Her daughter and best friend insist she needs a project to keep her occupied. Liz decides to share the beauty of Crystal Crescent

Beach with those who visit the beautiful east coast of Nova Scotia and prepares to embark on the adventure of her life. She moves into the converted art studio at the bottom of her garden and turns the old family home into The Crystal Crescent Inn.

One of her first visitors is famous archeologist, Merc MacGill, and he's not there to admire the view. The handsome bachelor believes there's an undiscovered eighteenth-century farmstead hidden inside the creeks and coves of Crystal Crescent, and Liz wants to help him find it.

But it's not all smooth sailing at the inn that overlooks the historic Sambro Lighthouse. No one has realized it yet, but the lives of everyone in Liz's family are intertwined with those first settlers who landed in Nova Scotia over two hundred and fifty years ago. Will they be able to unravel the mystery? Will the lives of Liz's two children be changed forever if they discover the link between the lighthouse and their old home?

Take a trip to Crystal Crescent Beach and join Liz, her family, and guests as they navigate the storms and calm waters of life and love under the watchful eye of the lighthouse and its secret.

ABOUT THE AUTHOR

Sylvia Price

Now an Amazon bestselling author, Sylvia Price is an author of Amish and contemporary romance and women's fiction. She especially loves writing uplifting stories about second chances!

Sylvia was inspired to write about the Amish as a result of the enduring legacy of Mennonite missionaries in her life. While living with them for three weeks, they got her a library card and encouraged her to start reading to cope with the loss of television and radio, giving Sylvia a new-found appreciation for books.

Although raised in the cosmopolitan city of Montréal, Sylvia spent her adolescent and young adult years in Nova Scotia, and the beautiful countryside landscapes and ocean views serve as the backdrop to her contemporary novels.

After meeting and falling in love with an American while living abroad, Sylvia now resides in the US. She spends her days writing, hoping to inspire the next generation to read more stories. When she's not writing, Sylvia stays busy making sure her three young children are alive and well-fed.

Subscribe to Sylvia's newsletter at newsletter.sylviaprice.com to stay in the loop about new releases, freebies, promos, and more. As a thank-you, you will receive several FREE exclusive short stories that aren't available for purchase!

Learn more about Sylvia at amazon.com/author/sylviaprice and goodreads.com/sylviapriceauthor.

Follow Sylvia on Facebook at facebook.com/sylviapriceauthor for updates.

Join Sylvia's Advanced Reader Copies (ARC) team at arcteam.sylviaprice.com to get her books for free before they are released in exchange for honest reviews.

Made in the USA
Monee, IL
06 October 2023